Landscapes of

ANDALUCIA

and the Costa del Sol

a countryside guide

John and Christine Oldfield

SUNFLOWER BOOKS

First published 1999
by Sunflower Books™
12 Kendrick Mews
London SW7 3HG, UK

ISBN 1-85691-127-6

El Pinarillo (Alternative walk 1(

Important note to the reader

We have tried to ensure that the descriptions and maps in this book ar
error-free at press date. The book will be updated, where necessary
whenever future printings permit. It will be very helpful for us to receiv
your comments (sent in care of the publishers, please) for the updatin
of future printings.

   We also rely on those who use this book — especially walkers — t
take along a good supply of common sense when they explore
Conditions change fairly rapidly in Andalucía, and ***storm damage c
bulldozing may make a route unsafe at any time***. If the route is not a
we outline it here, and your way ahead is not secure, return to the poin
of departure. ***Never attempt to complete a tour or walk und
hazardous conditions!*** Please read carefully the Country code on page
7-8, the Walking notes on pages 47-52, and the introductory commen
at the beginning of each tour and walk (regarding road condition
equipment, grade, distances and time, etc). Explore ***safely***, while at th
same time respecting the beauty of the countryside.

Cover photograph: El Torcal (Picnic CT4)
Title page: Cortijo de Buena Vista (Walk 12)

Photographs: John Oldfield
Maps: John Underwood, based on 1:25,000 and 1:50,000 maps of th
   Instituto Geográfico Nacional and the Servicio del Ejército
A CIP catalogue record for this book is available from the British Librar
Printed and bound in the UK by Brightsea Press, Exeter

10 9 8 7 6 5 4 3 2 1

Contents

Below: The Vega de Granada, with the snow-capped peak of Cerro de Caballo in the distance (Car tour 2)

☀ Preface _____

If you are not excited by Andalucía, you have no heart. At least, that is what is said. But we are convinced that you, our readers, *will* be excited after just the merest glimpse of the Andalucía that we know and love.

It is a land of contrasts, from bustling cities with great historical past and grand architecture to sleepy little villages and crumbling *cortijos* where goats graze and *campesinos* toil in the fields. The countryside is just as diverse. The magnificent Sierra Nevada and other snow-capped mountains tower over verdant valleys. Rivers tumble through gorges and snake across the landscape creating fertile plains, but there are also sierras that are barren and land that is parched and desolate.

To capture your imagination and fire your soul there are the vibrant colours of Andalucía. Reflecting the Spanish flag are the reds and golds of autumn leaves and berries along with the sunshine yellow of gorse, broom and mimosa. For Andalucía's own flag there is the green of the grass, trees and shrubs, together with the brilliant white of fairytale villages and snowy mountains. And we mustn't leave out the vivid blue of the sky and of reservoirs, rivers and the sea … or the abundant wildflowers of every hue.

During the latter stages of writing this book, as we sat basking in the warm sun by a hilltop *cortijo* contemplating these sparkling images and watching four eagles frolicking above, we shared the unspoken thought that life doesn't get much better than this.

We no longer live in Spain, but visit as often as possible this unique region whose Tourist Department slogan is *Andalucía, solo hay una*! There is only one!

Nature notes

As you travel through this area of Spain, and read our text, there are certain natural features which will frequently catch your attention. Some are explained below.

Alcornoque Cork oak tree, abundant throughout Andalucía. Its wood, hard and resistant, is fashioned into barrels and tools, and its acorns are used for animal feed. But principally it provides cork. Once stripped of the cork bark, contact with the sun turns the yellowish-coloured trunk a vivid red for a while — spectacular to behold, but not to be touched unless you fancy stained fingers.

Algarrobo Carob or locust tree. Common on many of the walks, its presence is usually announced by heaps of fallen pods around the base of the trunk. Large and brown and sometimes called St John's bread, the pods contain a sweet nutritious pulp said to be the honey eaten by St John the Baptist. The fruit is used in the preparation of a chocolate substitute and the seeds are supposed to have been the origin of the carat weight.

Cabra montés Translates literally as mountain goat but is actually the Spanish ibex, with characteristic long straight horns (see photograph page 2). Small herds roam the Andalusian mountains, particularly in the Parque Natural Sierra de las Nieves, where fences and grids keep them from straying off the hillsides. Look for them silhouetted majestically against the skyline or springing nimbly across the slopes. Most likely to be spotted or heard around November, the rutting season, when they are in frolicsome mood.

Cañada Gully or ravine, recognized in the past as a drove road or right of way for animals. Often clearly marked on Spanish topographical maps by a double dotted line and looking invitingly like a good track. Herdsmen may once have moved their livestock along these *cañadas,* but few of them are suitable for walkers. Do not be tempted to try them.

Pinsapo *Abies pinsapo Boiss,* the Spanish fir (sometimes known as hedgehog fir), a tree whose dark blue-green branches sprout huge bright green buds in spring. Over the centuries numbers have declined, and it is now confined solely to the mountains of Andalucía, particularly within the natural parks of the Nieves and Grazalema sierras. Ancient and majestic, it is variously referred to as the jewel, the king or the emblem of the natural parks — and deservedly so.

Pinsapos *in the Cañada del Cuerno (Walk 20)*

Vultures The Parque Natural de la Sierra de Grazalema supports the largest breeding colony of griffon vultures in Europe. They are gregarious birds and you will see groups soaring and circling above as you drive or walk in the park. The black vulture, an endangered species, is present in much smaller numbers and is usually seen solitary or in pairs. One of the world's largest birds, with a wingspan of almost 3m, it is a sight to remember.

Country code for walkers, motorists and picnickers

The Spanish countryside is essentially unspoiled. Only around the more accessible, and therefore popular, picnic or camping areas is there a litter problem. Please do not be tempted to add to it. Fire is a major hazard in countryside that is always parched during the summer months and sometimes all year round after a drought. Smokers must be particularly careful. Respect the country code and ensure that this beautiful area remains unspoiled.

- **Do not light fires or throw away lighted cigarette ends.**
- **Protect all wild or cultivated plants.** Don't pick wild flowers. Never cross cultivated land and do not be tempted to pick fruits, almonds or olives as these are clearly someone's private property.
- **Do not disturb or frighten animals or birds.**
- **Keep to designated paths.** Erosion is a problem in many mountain areas, and much of it is caused by over-zealous walkers taking shortcuts.

■ **Walk quietly through farms and hamlets.**

■ **Take all your litter away with you.**

■ **Protect water sources.** *Fuentes* (springs) in the mountains are especially important. When attending to 'calls of nature' keep well away from springs and streams and make sure that you bury all paper.

■ **Walkers — do not take risks!** *Never walk alone* and *always* tell someone where you are going and when you expect to return. It might be helpful also to leave this information on a note in your hotel room and/or in your parked car. Remember that any route could become dangerous after storms. If you are lost or injured you may have to wait a long time for help.

Language

Many people on the tourist beat speak English, but since that is not the case in the villages, a simple Spanish phrase book or pocket dictionary can be invaluable. It is useful to know some of the common Spanish words which crop up frequently in a countryside context. Some of them appear in the text *(in italics)*, and you will rapidly become familiar with them. They are listed in the glossary below, along with some other words that you may encounter on your travels.

Glossary

acequia narrow water channel

algarrobo carob tree

alcornoque cork oak

arroyo stream

autovía dual carriageway

ayuntamiento town hall

baño bath

barranco gorge, ravine or gully, usually dry

bocadillo sandwich

buho owl

burro donkey

cabra montés Spanish ibex

calle street

camino small street or path

cantera quarry

cañada gully, ravine or right of way

carretera main road

casa/casita house/ little house

casa consistorial town hall

cerro hill

collado mountain pass or saddle

correos post office

cortijo Andalusian farmhouse

coto privado de caza private hunting reserve

cueva cave

embalse reservoir

ermita chapel, shrine

finca farmhouse and farm

fuente spring

gasoleo diesel

gasolina petrol

hostal cheap hotel

jamón serrano cured ham

junta council

lavadero wash-house

merendero snack bar/basic country restaurant

mirador viewpoint

molino mill

nieve snow

parque park

peñón rock

pinsapo Spanish fir

playa beach

plaza square

puerto mountain pass or sea port

refugio mountain hut

río river

seco dry

tapas snacks or appetizers

toro bull

torre watchtower

vega plain

venta roadside restaurant

zona recreativa official picnic area with facilities

● Picnicking

In contrast to many other parts of Spain, there seem to be few official picnic areas in Andalucía. Those we found, designated by ⩗ in the text and on the maps, are generally attractive and well laid out, but very busy at weekends and *fiestas*. But who *needs* benches and bins? It's not too difficult to find secluded and spectacular alternatives. All the information you need to locate some of our favourite spots is detailed below. *Picnic numbers correspond to walk numbers* (except those at the end of the list, prefixed 'CT', and specific to a Car tour). You can quickly find their general location by looking at the maps where the precise location of each picnic site is indicated by *P*. Remember when you park your car never to block a road or track.

Although one or two of the sites are close to the road, others involve an interesting short walk, and sometimes some ascent or descent. Be sure to read the full description and equip yourself with all you might need, for example stout walking shoes, sunhat, suncream and ground sheet. You will sometimes have access to a *fuente*, but do not rely on this as your only water supply.

Most of our chosen spots are close to rivers, streams or reservoirs, and many enjoy spectacular mountain views. Nature lovers will delight in the variety of trees and shrubs, the abundance of wildflowers and the company of birds, both great and small. And of course the air is fresh.

All picnickers should observe the country code on pages 8-9.

1a OLD MILL AT BUSQUISTAR (map page 54)

⩗ to Busquístar (Car tour 1); 20min on foot. Follow Walk 1 as far as the river bed. Picnic by the water in this picturesque spot, then stroll along the old *acequia* as far as the dam and the clear pools. There is shade if you want it and a lovely ambience.

1b CORTIJOS DE PANJUILA (map page 54)

⩗ to Cortijos de Panjuila (Car tour 1); 13min on foot. Follow Walk 1 from the 1h21min point down to the *baños*. Fill water bottles from the *fuente* and sit on the rocks or in the shade just beyond the ruins, water cascading below. Enjoy the delightful panorama of brilliantly-white villages dotted all over the hillside in front of you.

1c FUENTE AGRIA (map page 54) ⩗

⩗ to just beyond Pórtugos (Car tour 1); no walking. A pretty site with an *ermita* and mineral springs just to the left of it (but the water tastes quite bitter). Sit on the benches or by the stream. Mature trees provide shade.

3 PUENTE BUCHITE (map page 59)

🚍 to Capileira (Car tour 1); 25min descent on foot. Follow Walk 3 as far as the bridge over the Poqueira River. A marvellous setting, in a deep gorge, with shady trees, fast-flowing clear water and rocks to sit on.

5a RIO CHICO FROM ORGIVA (map page 70)

🚍 to the old petrol station outside Orgiva (Car tour 1); 12min minimum on foot. Follow Walk 5 to the riverside and beyond — to any spot that takes your fancy. Attractive setting with plenty of rocks to settle on and clear flowing water. Very little shade. Opportunity for a leisurely stroll upriver as far as the little village of Bayacas, shown on page 17.

5b RIO CHICO FROM CARATAUNAS (map page 70)

🚍 to the Carataunas junction, 6km from Orgiva (Car tour 1); 18min minimum descent on foot. Follow Short walk 5-2 to the river bed. Turn downstream and select one of the many attractive spots with shade, rocks to sit on and running water.

6 ESTACION DE SAN JUAN (map pages 72-73)

🚍 to the 45km-point on Detour 2 of Car tour 2; 43min on foot — or 30min if you drive along the (very narrow) tramway to the Bar Chiquito. Follow Short walk 6, or else walk along the tramway in both directions. This wild spot at the end of the tramway offers a fast-flowing river, pools, steep rocks and cliffs, shade or sun as you wish and the opportunity to potter about by the waterside in a wonderful setting.

7 RUTA DE LAS SABINAS (map pages 72-73)

🚍 to the 38km-point on Detour 2 of Car tour 2; 11 or 16min walking. Park off the road at the bend and take the track going to the right, following Walk 7. (a) At 11min, at a junction, take the middle track which rises slightly to a small charming cabin, Cabaña Frasquita de Las Puentes. It is used as a weekend retreat but not signed as private. When no one is there it is a lovely spot with shade, a bench, and lots of atmosphere amongst the pines. (b) At 16min there is a lookout spot at the two wagon wheels. No shade but far-reaching views up the valley to the fantastic Sierra Nevada ridge.

8 PUENTE DE LOS SIETE OJOS (map pages 78-79)

🚍 to the 11.7km-point on Detour 1 of Car tour 2; 25min on foot. Follow Alternative walk 8 from the 15min-point (the car park) to the 40min-point. This tranquil spot at the Bridge of the Seven Eyes offers views of Cerro Gordo rising on one side and Trevenque towering majestically above the other. An *acequia* starts nearby and a convenient flat area, shaded by trees, overlooks the clear flowing river.

12 FABRICA DE LA LUZ (map page 94) 🎪

🚍 to the old church of Santa Ana in Canillas de Albaida (Car tour 3); 46min or 28min easy walking. Follow Walk 12 to the 46min-point (28min if you drive to the junction). Choose your spot at this well laid out *zona recreativa,* with picnic benches, shade and toilets. Enjoy the sound of a flowing stream, stunning mountain scenery and midweek tranquility. Short walk 2 describes a delightful stroll upriver from here.

14 PARQUE NATURAL MONTES DE MALAGA (map page 103)

🚍 to the Torrijos recreation area (Car tour 4); 13, 35 or 46min on foot. Follow Walk 14b. (a) At 13min you reach the ruins of Cortijo Pacheco Bajo, an old farmhouse with an *era* below. There are rocks to sit on and trees offer shade. You will marvel at the extent and variety of the woodland here. (b) At 35min the road crosses the Arroyo de los Malgarejos. Choose sun or shade and sit on the wall or on rocks up on the left, with cool fresh water cascading by. (c) At 46min you come to an open grassy area alongside the ruins of Santillana (photograph page 100). By the flowing stream there are convenient rocks and shady willows.

15 ERMITA DEL CALVARIO (map page 106)

🚐 or 🚌 to Mijas (Car tour 5); 16min on foot, on a steep but easy zigzag path. Follow Walk 15 up to the *ermita*. A bench on the little patio is in full sun, but the rocks on the surrounding slopes are shaded by pines. Encircled by the Sierra de Mijas, you have magnificent and far-reaching views over the village and agricultural land to the coast.

17 FINCA MANZAH AL KAID (map page 113)

🚐 or 🚌 to Marbella (Car tour 6); 16-19min on foot. Follow Walk 17 to the 16min-point. Picnic in the open area by the waterside or go a little further upstream and choose an even nicer spot — but stop short of the line of beehives. After rain you'll need a ground sheet to sit on. Surrounded by mountains and with fresh running water and shady trees, you could not ask for a more pleasant setting.

19a RIO DEL BURGO (map pages 120-121, photograph page 41)

🚌 to El Burgo (Car tour 6); 31-38min on foot. Follow Walk 19 to the 31min-point (above the weir). Picnic here in full sun on the rocky promontory, or go down the chained-off track to picnic by the waterside in the shade of trees. Have a paddle or even a bathe and enjoy the tranquillity.

19b LA FUENSANTA (map pages 120-121) 🏕

🚌 to the Fuensanta track just south of El Burgo (Car tour 6); 36min on foot — or no walking at all if you drive along the track.
If you avoid weekends, you may well have this enchanting picnic/camping area to yourself. Benches are set in woodland on the banks of the Arroyo de la Fuensanta, where a restored mill provides a picturesque focal point. A shrine to the Virgen de las Nieves adorns its entrance, and a courtyard boasts toilet and shower cubicles alongside a *fuente* with four spouts.

21 PUERTO DEL BOYAR (map pages 130-131)

🚌 to the *merendero*, just beyond Puerto del Boyar (Car tour 7); no walking or a 10min climb requiring stout footwear. Go through the gate to the left of the *merendero* and sit on the concrete walls by the water, source of the Río Guadalete. Alternatively — and preferably — continue, following Walk 21 from the 45min-point up to the level grassy area and choose your spot among the shady pines. There's a viewpoint just a few minutes along the path with rocks to sit on, a backdrop of rugged cliffs and a spectacular outlook over the Puerto — definitely worth the climb.

22 ARROYO DEL PAJARITO (map pages 130-131)

🚌 to Benaocaz (Car tour 7); 24min on foot from the church. Follow Short walk 2 down the cobbled trail to the bridge. Sit on rocks by the waterside with trees providing shade. A convoy of donkeys, loaded with milk churns, passes this way several times a day on its way to and from Cortijo del Puerto where the goats are milked.

23 RIO EL BOSQUE (map pages 130-131, photograph page 46)

🚌 to Benamahoma (follow directions on page 139 to get to Walk 23); up to 14min on foot. Follow Walk 23 for as long as you like. There are numerous attractive and secluded spots, but we suggest especially the area around the second ruined mill where there is open space, shady trees, flowing water, grass and rocks. Sit quietly and you'll be entertained by the song and flight of lively little birds and, if you're *really* lucky, you might see an otter.

CT1a LA POZA (see the touring map)

🚗 to the 60km point. Park in Pampaneira's public car park; 15min on foot. Walk down from the main square to the road above the electricity station which comes into sight below. Turn right on a rough path which follows the river upstream. Mostly wide, with just a few narrow sections, it undulates above spectacular falls and pools to an attractive bridge and a dam. Known as La Poza, this former official picnic site was ravaged by floods, and now only the benchtops are visible above the silt. But with a flowing river, a *fuente*, grass and rocks to sit on, tall poplars providing a bit of shade and views down the valley, it's a lovely spot for Landscapers.

CT1b THE ROOF OF SPAIN (see the touring map)

🚗 to Capileira. Follow the optional drive up the Sierra Nevada road to the track; 6min on foot. Walk along the track until it opens out on the right to a gently sloping area of grass and rocks with low trees which provide limited shade. From this high vantage point views are absolutely stunning. Veleta (3398m) dominates the Sierra Nevada ridge, towering above and covered with snow until around April, while the coastal sierras line up below like a geographical model. Three villages, sparkling in the sunshine, complete the awe-inspiring picture.

CT1c TREVELEZ (see the touring map and photograph page 19)

🚗 to Trevélez (Car tour 1); no walking or up to 6min on foot. Park near the bridge and picnic by the river. Spots in the open close to the bridge are popular, but it's much better to take the little path that goes upstream *before* the bridge. Tempting sites begin to appear immediately, but in about 6min the valley narrows; here rocks and pools make the perfect stopping-point. Secluded, with sun and shade.

CT2 EMBALSE DE LOS BERMEJALES (see the touring map)

🚗 to the 128km point; no walking. Sit among the pines, with the reservoir shimmering before you, then take a stroll along the water's edge.

CT3a LA RAHIJE (see the touring map) 🏕

🚗 to the 66.8km point; no walking. This picnic/camping spot, set on shady slopes just alongside the road, is in wild countryside in the middle of nowhere and almost deserted during the week. Choose one of the secluded benches or sit by the side of the river near a little waterfall.

CT3b EMBALSE DE VIÑUELA (see the touring map)

🚗 to the 85.6km point; 6 to 10min on foot. Take the track which leads to the old *cortijo* and choose your spot. Sit on the rocks under the shady tree in front of the *cortijo,* or go a little further and picnic just by the water's edge. There is little shade and no drinking water, but the stunning views of the interesting mountains which circle the reservoir make it an unforgettable spot.

CT4 EL TORCAL (see the touring map and photograph opposite)

🚗 to the 63.2km point; 2 to 30min walking. Follow the waymarked trail. You are spoiled for choice of picnic site in this *parque natural,* but one of the best is in an open meadow about halfway round the trail. Dwarfed by the towering rocky sculptures shown opposite (which provide adequate shade) and carpeted with delicate wild flowers, this is a wonderland of images. Scan the skies and you may spot griffon vultures soaring overhead.

CT6a PARQUE NATURAL SIERRA DE LAS NIEVES: CONEJERAS (see the touring map)

🚗 to the 47km point. Drive for 2 km along the good track to the Conejeras notice board by a stream bed; no walking. Sit on rocks and enjoy the wildness of this place. There's limited shade but spectacular surroundings. Tackle the short walking trail detailed on the notice board.

CT6b MIRADOR DE ISTAN (see the touring map)

🚌 or 🚗 to Istán (detour on Car tour 6); 8min on foot. Follow our *walk* suggestion at the end of this detour. There is no shade, but there are benches in the rocks, and the views are superb. The *embalse* glistens in the sunshine and draws the eye all the way down the valley to the coast.

The waymarked walk at El Torcal (Picnic CT4)

Touring

Andalucía is a vast region. You could spend a lifetime investigating the architectural and historical legacy of its chequered past and another lifetime exploring its mountains and river valleys. A few car tours can scarcely do it justice, but we have tried to ensure that you see the most representative features and experience at first hand the vital and vibrant nature of this land.

Car tour 7 starts from Ronda, but all the others start from the coast and can easily be picked up at intermediate points if you wish. Apart from the main north to south arteries, roads through the mountains are narrow and winding. Take great care, always expecting the *unexpected*. Uncharacteristically heavy storms in the late 1990s caused considerable structural damage both to major and minor roads, resulting in complete road closures or lengthy delays. Most repairs should now be complete, but there is always a possibility of it happening again. Road numbering seems to be in a permanent state of flux, so many numbers on commercial maps are wrong. The few road numbers we have mentioned on our map and in the touring notes were correct at the time of writing.

You will derive little pleasure from the tours if you rush from place to place trying to pack in as much as possible in a short time. So, if possible, **allow a full day for each tour**, to ensure plenty of time to stop and explore as the fancy takes you. The scenery is so breathtaking that it should be savoured at leisure. Allow plenty of time, too, for the deservedly famous tourist attractions like the Cueva de Nerja, the Alhambra in Granada and Ronda's spectacular Tajo Gorge. And while the little white villages dotted all over

Salares, a typical pueblo blanco *(Car tour 3)*

Bridge at Salares, the village shown opposite (Car tour 3)

the mountainsides are enchanting, you will have to park and go on foot to visit them: *don't* attempt to drive through their concreted narrow streets! Try to make time on each tour to do at least one of the short walks that we suggest and look out for the starting points of the longer walks, perhaps to be tackled another day.

Our touring notes are brief; we give only the minimum of historical or other information that you can find in standard guides or free tourist office leaflets. Instead we place emphasis on times and distances, road conditions and possibilities for sightseeing, **picnicking** and **walking**. The driving times assume driving always within the speed limit, but do *not* allow for any stops. Beware: short distances can often take much longer than expected. **The pull-out touring map is designed to be held out opposite the touring notes**; the **symbols** in the map key correspond to those in the text. There are plenty of **petrol stations** on the main roads, but fewer in the mountains. They are always well signposted and usually open during normal business hours.

When touring always **carry plenty of water**. Although all the towns and some of the villages you will pass through have bars, they are not necessarily just where you need them. Bars that don't provide full meals usually have a selection of *tapas* or can make up a sandwich *(bocadillo)*, but it's really much better to plan on picnicking in the fresh air at one of the spots we suggest. Bars and petrol stations are likely to have **toilets** and **telephone**.

Much of your touring will be at high altitude, and the air will be chilly even outside winter. Take **warm clothing** so that you can leave your car in comfort. Whatever the time of year, the sun can be strong, so **suncream and head covering** are essential if you intend to walk around.

Before you set off, *do* read the **Nature notes** on pages 6-7 and skim over the **Glossary** on page 8. And **please observe the Country code on pages 7-8.**

1 THE ALPUJARRA

Almuñécar • Salobreña • Orgiva • Pampaneira • Bubión • Capileira • Pitres • Pórtugos • Trevélez • Vélez de Benaudalla • Almuñécar

173km/107mi; 4h-4h30min driving

On route: ⊞ at Fuente Agria, Capileira; Picnics (see **P** symbol and pages 9-13): 1a-c, 3, 5a, 5b, CT1a-c; Walks 1-5

The Alpujarra, an exquisite area of mountains and river valleys, extends from the south face of the Sierra Nevada all the way to the Mediterranean. It was the last stronghold of the Moors in Andalucía, and many traces of their occupation still remain today. It is here that you will find the best examples of Berber architecture. whitewashed houses, built in layers, each have a flat roof and distinctive chimney. Tinaos, or galleries, provide passage from house to house and between levels, and walls and balconies are festooned with colourful flowers in equally colourful pots. The Moors also developed a formidable system of acequias (water channels) to irrigate the land, and some are still in use today in market gardens and orchards. The Alpujarra is a botanist's dream, reputed to boast the highest number of unique species of flora in the world. Discover some of these for yourself by following the walks referred to in this tour.

From the roundabout by the bus station in **Almuñécar** (♍️⬛⬛✖️⌨️⊕) follow the N340 (signposted to Motril) east along the coast. This is a heavily built-up route, but hills rise quite close to the road on the landward side and in places steep cliffs drop down to the sea. Every so often their line is broken by delightful little coves and watch-towers *(torres)* standing sentinel above. The road winds across deep *barrancos,* with views of long-abandoned terracing on the slopes. Near the km324 road marker the small town of Salobreña comes into sight, built around the skirts of its ancient castle. In times past, the castle was used as a royal summer residence and also as a prison. Below, stretching towards the sea, is a fertile plain where sugar cane and cumin used to be the main crops. Pass the exit for Salobreña★ (12km ♍️⬛⬛✖️) — worth a visit, perhaps another day. Cross the plain and join the N323 to Granada (15km). If there is any snow lying on the high peaks of the Sierra Nevada, you will soon catch sight of it as the road heads directly towards the mountains, past fields of soft fruit, bananas and flowers. Pass a petrol station (19km ⌨️) and follow the wide Río Guadalfeo, a main fluvial artery of the Alpujarra, through a spectacular gorge. After a few minutes (25km ⌨️) you will see, over on the right, the rectangular Moorish tower of Vélez de Benaudalla.

At 30km, almost immediately after the road crosses the river, turn right across a bridge, following signposting to Orgiva. (The road continuing straight on goes to Granada; Car tour 2.) You are now on a narrower and winding road,

Bayacas is one of the little villages encountered on Walk 5, which begins near Orgiva

with the river still on your left. At the time of writing, a reservoir, the Presa de Rules, was under construction here. Drive high above the river, with cliffs on the right, until eventually Orgiva comes into view, tucked in at the foot of the high peaks. Turn left (42.6km), cross the river on the bridge known locally as the Puente de los Siete Ojos ('Bridge of the Seven Eyes'), and reach **Orgiva★** (44km ✝ ▲ ✕ ☗ ⊕△). This town, at a height of 450m, is considered the capital of the Western Alpujarra and has great historic associations. The church, with impressive twin bell towers, dates from 1580 and is on the site of an old mosque. The valley around Orgiva is home to majestic olive trees, hundreds of years old, their trunks contorted with the passage of time.

Drive through the town and follow the road as it turns sharp left before the church. Just before the bridge, you pass the old petrol station (45.4km ☗), starting point for Walk 5 which meanders up a charming valley (*P*5a) to Carataunas, a village which you will pass close to a little later. Note that this petrol station may be out of business when you come here, as a new one has been built just beyond the next junction, where you turn right (46km ☗) towards Bubión and Trevélez. This minor road winds up steadily into the Alpujarra, providing magnificent views across mountains and valleys and the numerous little white settlements dotted around the slopes.

With the Río Chico down to the right, keep on the main road, ignoring turn-offs to various restaurants. Ignore, too, the turn to Carataunas (52km ✕) — unless you wish to take a short walk by a stream or have a picnic (*P*5b, Short walk 5). At 54.5km you pass the Ermita del Padre Eterno; it stands on a bend, at a junction where a forestry track *(camino forestal)* winds up into the Sierra Nevada. Summits visible from around here will be snow-covered for much of the year, and the altitude ensures that some bright pink almond blossom lingers well into March.

Two villages come into sight, then another, higher up on the slopes ahead. The three of them, overlooking the Poqueira Valley and shining brilliant white against the hillside, are typical of the region. Cross the bridge over the Río Poqueira and, just beyond the electricity station (59km), notice a path going off to the left: it leads along the river to La Poza (*P*CT1a). Not far ahead is the first of the villages, **Pampaneira** (60km ♦♠♣✕M; photograph page 67), from where Walk 4 climbs an ancient trail to the next two villages on our route. On coming to a junction (62km ♨) turn left, to drive through **Bubión★** (♦♠♣✕♨) and reach **Capileira★** (67km ♦♠♣✕☞M). This village, shown on page 68, is a popular walking centre. In putting together Walks 2 and 3, both of which start here, we have tried to capture the best features of the surrounding area. Short walk 3, to a delightful picnic spot by the riverside (*P*3), will give you a tantalising taste, while Walk 2 is an exhilarating trek to the slopes of Mulhacén (photograph pages 62-63).

Possible detour: The main tour turns back from Capileira, but you might like to make a short (8km return) detour along the road ahead. This route eventually deteriorates to a track only suitable for 4WD vehicles, and it is only open for four months of the year. It climbs across the high peaks of the Sierra Nevada to the ski centre (which we approach from the other side on Detour 2 in Car tour 2). But if you have time it's worth driving the first part of it to enjoy the panoramic views. From the car park at the top of the village (⊼) continue up the steep winding road (Walk 4 follows this route, but turns down to Bubión after 0.8km). Park 4km uphill, at the point where a drivable track (which goes to Trevélez) turns off to the right; the junction is signed with a red and white GR marker on a post. Why not walk a short way along the track (*P*CT1b)?

The main tour continues from Capileira: we retrace our route through Bubión and turn left at the junction (72km). After passing a *mirador* (☞), drive round the head of the valley at Barranco de la Sangre and climb gradually past the right turn to Mecina (75km). Drive through **Pitres** (77km ♠♣✕△) and continue up into **Pórtugos** (79km ♠♣✕♨). A mulberry plantation was started here for the silk trade in the first half of the 20th century, and this industry thrived for some time. Just after leaving this town behind, you come to Fuente Agria (♦⊼*P*1c), mineral springs dating back to 1872. The five spouts are to be found just to the left of the pretty *ermita,* and people swear that the water gushing from each spout has different mineral properties. We're not sure about that, but can vouch for the fact that it all tastes quite bitter! Walk 1 nears its end here, after a wander through exceptionally beautiful countryside.

Continue to a fork at the entrance to **Busquístar** (81km ✝ ▲ ✕) and take the left-hand road signposted to Trevélez. To the right, the village itself is the start and end point of Walk 1 which leads to a lovely riverside picnic spot (**P**1a). Pass the Hostal Mirador (☎) and, as the mountains draw closer, you enter the Parque Natural Sierra Nevada. Trevélez comes into view, nestling in the valley with a snowy backdrop. At 85km, on a bend, don't miss the Barranco de los Alísos, a good spot for a break. A path, overgrown in places, but colourful in spring and affording tremendous mountain views, goes up to the left, just before the bridge, and leads to waterfalls and a pool.

Follow the Río Trevélez upstream, through countryside which looks especially magnificent in autumn. Descend

Picnic CT1c: many people picnic near the bridge at Trevélez, but there are more secluded spots a short way upriver, where this photograph was taken.

into **Trevélez★** (91km 🏠 ✕ 🛆), the highest settlement on the peninsula (1476m), and famous for its trout and *jamón serrano*, cured ham. Drive through the village overlooked by the magnificent peak of Peñabon and pause as you reach the head of the valley (*P*CT1c; photograph page 19).

Having crossed the bridge, look back across the river to Mulhacén, at 3482m continental Spain's highest peak. Notice, too, the chestnut trees along this spectacular route as the road now runs downriver, high above the water. At a crest (98.5km) turn right for Cástaras and Torviscón. Just before passing some distinctive rock formations, there is a helipad on the right: like the others placed strategically around the countryside, it is for use in case of fire or other emergency. Pass a series of old ruined buildings looking like barracks (102km) and probably associated with the mines nearby, then turn right at a junction signposted to Almería. Walk 1 comes up from the valley on the track by the *cortijo* on the corner, follows this road for a short way and then turns off at the little hamlet known as **Cortijos de Panjuila** (103km). Stretch your legs here by following a section of Walk 1 to another choice spot for a break (*P*1b).

After noting some disused mines over on the left, bear right at the next junction for Almegijar. Descend a little and pass the road to this village (108km), looking in spring for the tall asphodels growing along the verges. The road zigzags down into the valley, crossing the Río Guadalfeo again at 112km. Go right at the junction (114km) signed to Orgiva and **Torviscón** which you pass through at 115km (🏠 ✕). Surviving sections of the old road provide a glimpse of what travel in these parts used to be like.

Descend gradually, eventually rounding the head of a *barranco*, past Puerto Jubíle, set in a deep gorge forged out over centuries by the waters raging down from the Sierra Nevada. Beyond another helipad on the right, we reach the valley floor and a tunnel (130km). Ignore the right turn to Orgiva and retrace a short section of your outward route, passing the Presa de Rules. Don't cross the bridge (142km): instead turn left and drive through the long main street of **Vélez de Benaudalla** (144km ⛪🏠✕). You might like to stop and look at the beautiful garden created during the 13th-century Nazarí dynasty. Central to its theme is water, which spouts from fountains, tumbles down waterfalls and flows gently along *acequias*. At the very end of the village, take the narrow unsigned road which forks down to the right past a plaque. Turn left on the N323 and then right when you reach the coastal N340, back to Almuñécar (173km).

2 SIERRA NEVADA

Almuñécar • Salobreña • Puerto del Suspiro del Moro • Granada: the Alhambra • Armilla • Jayena • Otívar • Jete • Almuñécar

Without detours: 187km/116mi; 4h-5h driving; Detour 1: 23km/14mi, 40min driving; Detour 2: 63km/39mi, 2h driving

On route: ⚲ at La Zubia, Sierra Nevada Visitor Centre; Picnics (see **P** symbol and pages 9-13): 6, 7a, 7b, 8, CT2; Walks (5), 6-9

*No visit to Andalucía would be complete without taking in one of Spain's most famous cities and setting eyes on the long curved ridge of the Sierra Nevada which boasts the highest peak on the Iberian Peninsula, Mulhacén (3482m/11,420ft). This tour enables you to do just that, and the two **highly recommended** detours lead you to walks right in the heart of the mountains. Snow lies on the peaks for ten months of the year but, lower down, especially in spring, the slopes are carpeted with wildflowers, many endemic to the Sierra Nevada region. You may wish to spend time exploring the historic sights of Granada, content to gaze upon the high peaks of the Sierra Nevada from thirty kilometres away. Or perhaps you will feel drawn to walk in these imposing mountains. To fit in both will require more than just one day, so do some planning before setting off. Whatever you decide, it will be an unforgettable experience. The tour is particularly enjoyable in early spring, when there is still snow on the slopes and the weather is warm enough to be comfortable when you venture out of the car. Avoid Sundays and holidays when the roads, particularly on the detours, will be extremely busy.*

Follow Car tour 1 out of **Almuñécar** (⚲🏨🏕✕🚰⊕) as far as the bridge across the Río Guadalfeo (30km). Go straight ahead towards Granada on a newish stretch of dual carriageway. Pass the road to Lanjarón and Orgiva (46km), starting point for Walk 5 which meanders up the valley of the Río Chico. Your road passes through and around several small industrial and agricultural towns before crossing the Río Durcal (55km) and reaching the start of the Vega de Granada (57km 🚰). This vast, fertile and undulating agricultural plain stretches for many kilometres, and you'll see its main town, Padul, over on the left (59km). The road climbs steadily but gradually to **Suspiro del Moro** (67km) a pass at 860m. From here, the peaks of the Sierra Nevada are magnificent, even in summer when the snows have melted. The road becomes a motorway and you will soon see Granada spread out along the lower slopes ahead. A cloud of pollution often hangs over the city, contributing to its drab appearance and giving no hint of the splendours that await you there.

Ignore exits numbered 141 and 138. Take exit 135 (77km) for the Alhambra — the 'Ronda Sur' (southern ring road). *If you are going to take Detour 1 (page 23), take the second exit off the ronda (78km), signposted to La Zubia. Otherwise continue to follow the Alhambra signs into a* two-lane tunnel. *If you are going to take Detour 2 (page 25), keep to the right-hand lane now.* For the main tour take the left lane: you find yourself at the end of the dual carriageway and climbing a hill, with fantastic views over the valley. Pass the coach park and reach the **Alhambra★** (83km **ℹ**).

After your visit, turn back, so that you are driving towards the Sierra Nevada peaks. To explore Granada itself, turn right at the first junction. Otherwise, start the leisurely drive back to base, returning through the tunnel and taking the right-hand lane signposted to Jaén (89km). Exit almost immediately to **Armilla** on the C340 and enter this busy industrial town (91km ✖). Drive straight through and turn right at traffic lights (92km) for Churriana de la Vega and Malaha. Pass a petrol station on the left (93km ⛽) then an old disused airport. Go through **Las Gabias** (96km ♠✖⛽) and continue across the plain. For as far as the eye can see there are green fields and neat rows of trees — mainly olives, but with some almonds among them. Pass a karting centre on the right (100km) and wind steeply downhill with far-reaching views over terrain which is now much drier. Pass through **Malaha** (105km), a spa town with mineral springs. Its river is now virtually dry, all the water being diverted through a sophisticated irrigation system developed by the Arabs and still ensuring the agricultural success of the area.

You cross this section of plain on a long straight road, passing a petrol station (114km ⛽) just beyond the road to Escúzar. At 116km you come to the setting shown on pages 4-5, where the leftmost visible peak of the imposing ridge is Cerro de Caballo (3013m). Climb into the low hills at the edge of the plain and pass through the little village of **Agrón** (119km). Then descend (123km), with views over the Almijara ridge and then the Embalse de los Bermejales below. At a junction, turn left for Fornes and wind downhill through almond groves, towards the reservoir. A track (128km) leads to the waterside, where you could picnic on the high banks or take a stroll through the trees (***P***CT2).

Continue to the southern end of the reservoir, pass the turn to Fornes and drive on through the winding streets of **Jayena** (135km). After leaving this village and crossing the Río Grande (136km ⛽), the road undulates through olive groves. The road is little used — not surprising, since it does not appear on some maps. At a junction (146km) turn right (signposted to Almuñécar) and pass a bar/restaurant (147km ✖). The Almijara ridge extends impressively on the right, and the road passes a turn to a 'Granja Escuela' (Farm School; 154km).

Then suddenly — and completely unexpectedly — the landscape changes totally. Rounding a bend, the road starts contouring around steep cliffs and through a pass 1.2km/0.7mi long. The scenery is breathtaking and awe-inspiring, a sort of moonscape with rugged hills and deep valleys. But keep your eyes on the road as well: it is narrow and winding, and cars sometimes take the curves on the wrong side. Views become even more amazing as each bend unfolds. To the right is the Sierra de Almijara and, to the left, the Sierra del Chaparral. At the end of the pass you come 'back down to earth' (160km) and head through gentler terrain (162km 🗔 and ⛽ closed Sundays). Just beyond this lonely petrol station there is a *fuente* on the left with clear cold water straight from the mountains.

As the road continues to wind, notices ask you to sound your horn on the bends. Admire yet more majestic views from another *mirador* (🗔) and cross a bridge at the head of the valley. Notice Lentejí, a village high above, and drive through **Otívar** (174km ✗). Surrounding hill slopes are dark and heavily wooded, mainly with pines, *nísperos* (medlars) and *chirimoyas* (custard apples). The Río Verde comes into view on the right, and you follow it all the way to the coast, crossing it once.

Drive through **Jete** (178km) where there is a chapel in the rock dedicated to the Virgin of the Waters, pass a petrol station (181km ⛽) and, on the extreme outskirts of Almuñécar, reach signs inviting you to visit a fine Roman aqueduct★ (183km 🏛). It is definitely worth a stop and a leg-stretch, so park and take the steps which descend from the road. Then continue on into Almuñécar, arriving back at the roundabout at the bus station after 187km.

Detour 1: Ronda Sur • La Zubia • Fuente del Hervidero • Canal de la Espartera • Ronda Sur

From the Ronda Sur take the second exit (the 78km-point of the main tour) for **La Zubia** (🔺✗) and drive across the plain into this small town. Now follow signs for 'Cumbres Verdes': towards the end of the town the signs point you sharp left and then immediately right. This is the Huenes Valley road, and it climbs steadily through pine forests. There are picnic benches (🏕) amongst the trees — nicely laid out, but poorly maintained and often badly littered. After passing the **Cumbres Verdes** housing development (🔺✗), the road deteriorates somewhat but presents no driving problems.

Pine forests give way to open hill slopes and the **Fuente del**

Detour 1 and Walk 8: view to the Boca de la Pesca (on the right) from the Canal de la Espartera. Walk 9 would take you over 'Fish-Mouth'.

Hervidero, an isolated restaurant sitting amidst cultivated fields (10km ✕). Walks 8 and 9, both magnificent hikes, start from here. Why not take a half-hour break and enjoy some mountain air? Just park under the tree by the *fuente* and follow Walk 8 to the 15min-point, where you will have the tremendous view shown above. Or *drive* to the viewpoint by following the rest of the detour, but *beware of potholes!* From here the road bears left and, shortly afterwards, on a sharp left-hand bend, you'll spot a track rising to the right, to a parking area (11.7km). There are several signs here, some claiming it is private land. They are generally ignored and nobody seems to mind, but park just off the road if you wish. Whether you have come on foot or by car, you now enjoy fantastic views of the Alayos de Dílar, the crags overlooking the Dílar gorge. The rocky peak to the left of the crags is Trevenque (2079m), while just in front of you is an enclosed section of the **Canal de la Espartera**, an incredible feat of engineering which Walk 8 follows to its source. Short walk 8 continues along the dirt road to the Puente de los Siete Ojos ('Bridge of the Seven Eyes'; *P*8) set directly below Trevenque; Alternative walk 8 goes on from the bridge to get acquainted with the mountain from even closer quarters. To the right here are two buildings, one old and incomplete, the other a modern chalet, and a little lower down is the old Cortijo Sevilla. They make quite a picture with the Boca de la Pesca ('Fish-Mouth'; Walk 9) rising behind them.

Return to your car, wherever you left it, and drive back the way you came, enjoying even better views of Granada from this perspective. Turn right at the main road in La Zubia and drive out of the town and back onto the Ronda Sur at the roundabout (23km). Take the first exit, signposted to the Alhambra and Sierra Nevada. In the tunnel, take the left lane for the Alhambra and pick up the main tour again where you left it, or, for the second detour, take the right lane, signposted Sierra Nevada, which exits the Ronda Sur at the far end of the tunnel.

Detour 2: Ronda Sur • Sierra Nevada Visitor Centre • Prado Llano (ski village) • Maitena Visitor Centre • Güéjar Sierra • Alhambra approach road

Note: If you are not confident driving on rough, steep and narrow mountain roads with sheer drops to one side, plan to retrace your route from the Visitor Centre (37km), rather than completing the suggested circuit.

Take the right-hand lane through the tunnel at the 78km-point on the main tour and find yourself on the main Sierra Nevada road (A395) leading to the ski village. Ignore exits to various small towns and villages and wind high above the valleys. This good road was built in 1996 for the World Alpine Ski Championships. For a while the surroundings are well cultivated with olives and almonds, but as the altitude increases these groves give way to slopes that are either barren or covered in pines. There are several restaurants and hotels (▲▲ ✕) on the route, and from the Mirador de Canales (14km 📷) you can appreciate the wonderfully exotic scenery. Down in the valley on the left lies a reservoir, the Embalse de Canales. You will soon begin to see vestiges of snow on the higher slopes (18km �). Then, on a right hand bend, at a junction with the old road (19km), you come to the **Sierra Nevada Visitor Centre** (*i*) at a place known as El Desvío. Walk 7 starts near here and you will return to this point after visiting the ski village.

Continuing uphill, after rounding a bend (22km) you come face to face — during most of the year — with snow-clad mountains. The ski village soon comes into sight at the head of the valley, and the ski slopes on Veleta (3398m) are clearly visible. We run out of superlatives when attempting to describe the exhilarating scenery up here — you *must* see it for yourself! A *mirador* (📷) with a *fuente* (24km) allows you to stop and take it all in. Then you reach **Prado Llano**, the ski village (28km ▲▲ ✕), at an altitude of 2075m. There is a huge car park (paid parking and no caravans allowed). This enormous purpose-built village (photograph overleaf) is quite tastefully arranged around central pedestrian areas with shops, restaurants, bars and the ski schools and ticket offices. The residential buildings are piled in layers high up the hillside. It is worth exploring and getting good close-ups of the snowy slopes.

Leave the village (on the Granada road) and return to the Visitor Centre (37km). If you have decided *not* to follow the entire detour route, you can go straight back along the Granada road from here and rejoin the main tour at the 79km-point. (But if you would like to see the settings for Picnics 7a and 7b, you can carry on the further 1km with no problem.)

If you are game to carry on, leave the main road and drive up to the right, past the Visitor Centre; then fork left following signposting to the Seminario Sierra Nevada. Descend past several relatively young pine plantations and notice the village Güéjar Sierra across the valley to the left. As the road makes a hairpin bend to the left (38km), Walk 7 starts off on a track to the right and, on its way to the Collado de las Sabinas, passes two picnic

Prado Llano (Flat Pastures), the ski village, enjoys snow almost all year round.

spots (**P**7a, 7b), the second with fantastic views of the Sierra Nevada ridge.

Continue descending through pines and orchards, their blossom painting a colourful picture in early spring. The road soon becomes rough and potholed in places (40km), as you drive alongside some metal fencing and pass a *fuente* on the right and then a left turn to the Seminario and Hotel del Duque. There must be a story attached to this strange place, but we were unable to unearth it. Ignore a track to the right as the road hairpins to the left (42.3km) and you pass below the hotel. With sheer drops to the right and no improvement in the surface, the road now zigzags steeply downhill — *take great care.* Reach a *cortijo* (44km), with particularly resplendent blossom in March, and say hello to the donkey which is usually tethered here. A little further down you pass the green entry gate to the *cortijo* and keep zigzagging down to the Mesón Restaurante El Charcón on the banks of the Río Genil (44.6km).

There are a few other buildings on the banks of the river, and the route of an old tramway runs along the far side. The old tram used to carry people from the bustle of Granada to the Estación de San Juan, where they could enjoy a day out in spectacular countryside — a journey of some 20km, with a gain of almost 500m in altitude. Continue past the **Maitena Visitor Centre** (45km *i*). Walk 6 sets off from here and initially follows the tramline past the old Maitena Station, to where the fast-flowing Río Genil and surrounding rugged cliffs offer a dramatic picnic spot (**P**6) at the Estación de San Juan. The walk then continues upriver on the Camino de la Estrella (Pathway to the Star); photographs page 74) for unforgettable views of the Sierra Nevada ridge.

To continue the tour, cross the bridge over the Río Genil and bear left. Go through two tunnels and fork right at the next junction, where a restaurant lies to the left (✕). Climb steeply, high above the valley, to a *mirador* (📷) with extensive views over the Genil Valley and the long thin Embalse de Canales. On reaching the large village of **Güéjar Sierra** (48km ✚✕) follow a signpost indicating a sharp left turn for Granada. As you leave the village, now on a proper road (sigh of relief!), notice the amazing pinnacles towering over on the left. Continue past orchards and the village of Pinos Genil, high above the reservoir. Turn right for Granada (56.7km; signposted) and drive along a pleasant tree-lined road. At the next major junction (59.1km), go straight ahead through **Lancha de Cenes**. Fork right for the Alhambra (63km) and pick up the main tour at about the 80km-point.

3 THE AXARQUIA

Cueva de Nerja • Frigiliana • Cómpeta • Canillas de Albaida • Salares • Canillas de Aceituno • Puente Don Manuel • Vélez Málaga • Torre del Mar • Torrox Costa • Cueva de Nerja

128km/79mi; 3h-4h driving

On route: ⊞ at La Rajihe; Picnics (see **P** symbol and pages 9-13): 12, CT3a-b; Walks 10-13

This varied and interesting tour circles the part of the province of Málaga referred to as the Axarquía, from the arabic word for 'eastern zone'. Sheltered from the cold and the winds by the Sierras de Tejeda y Almijara, it enjoys a balmy climate which the Arabs exploited by introducing sugar cane and wine and initiating the agricultural traditions of the area. As a result, trading prospered, with export of goods such as silk, raisins, figs, almonds, oil, wine and sugar. Tall chimneys of the many old sugar mills can still be seen today. In this rural environment, do not be surprised to meet flocks of sheep and goats on the road. On the circuit you will notice, from different angles, a village perched on top of a hill. This 'balcón de la Axarquia' is Comares, which boasts a 16th-century church and the ruins of its ancient castle.

Start from the **Cueva de Nerja★** (signposted with a circular maze) — just north of the N340, close to Maro. This vast cave, discovered by children in 1959, is one of the most beautiful in Europe. Special features are the 32m-high pillar in one of the chambers and wall paintings from the Stone Age. Walk 10 starts here and climbs high into the mountains, while the short and alternative walks stick to lower terrain.

Drive down the road to the N340 and turn right. Almost immediately pass on your right the Puente de Aguila: this four-tier aqueduct is a 19th-century replica of the great aqueduct in Segovia. Proceed along the fertile coast with orchards, some under cover as protection from the elements, before passing along the upper reaches of **Nerja** (2.5km ⛺🏔✕🛒⊕). Cross the Río Chillar (4.5km; photograph page 91) and turn right for Frigiliana, leaving behind the bustle of the coastal strip. The Río Chillar is deep down on the right as the road climbs steadily towards the sierras, with the conical peak of Cielo distinctive in the distance.

You pass a little huddle of houses and the Restaurante Molinete on the right (8.6km ✕). These are on the return route of Walk 11 which starts in Nerja at the mouth of the Chillar and takes a circuitous route over hills and valleys to Frigiliana. Even at this short distance from the coast, mountains dominate the landscape. A right fork (9km) takes you into **Frigiliana★** (⛺🏔✕). At a height of 435m, this typically picturesque and brilliantly whitewashed mountain village was the last in the area to be abandoned by the Moors. The road winds through the main street to the spot at the head of the valley where the tourists congregate around a few bars, restaurants and shops. Bear left here, past the bus stop, then fork right (where the left fork goes back to Nerja). You are now contouring round the valley on a road (not shown on some maps) lined with palm trees. But we call it the 'mimosa road', because in spring mimosas provide huge splashes of yellow all the way along.

Frigiliana

The surrounding slopes are neatly planted with fruit trees, as the road climbs gradually, passing the bar/restaurante Santo Cristo (✕) and winding high above Frigiliana. There are several more restaurants along the route, all commanding awesome views over the countryside. Traversing a short ridge (15km) you can see down into the valleys on both sides, with the high peaks of the Almijara looking mystical in the morning haze. To the right, the Reserva Nacional de Sierra de Tejeda extends to Salares and beyond. Start descending (19km) and catch sight of the huge bulk of Maroma (2065m) at the far end of the Sierra de Tejeda. It is the highest peak in the area, and vestiges of snow linger into early spring. Wind down through fertile slopes to a dip (23.5km), then bear right up to a junction. Turn left and take the higher of two roads, lined with eucalyptus trees. Descend to the next junction (24.5km) and turn right on the MA102, signposted to Cómpeta. To the left is Torrox (♁ ▲ ✕), a town which claims to have the best climate in Europe.

The road, bumpy in places, skirts the hillsides, gradually gaining altitude. On the left, across the *barranco*, the slopes are dotted with villas, *cortijos* and water tanks, all startlingly whitewashed. You are now entering wine country, with neatly planted vineyards. Close to many of the *cortijos* you will also notice small rectangular plots laid out side by side on the sloping inclines; they look like large graves with triangular headstones. These are *paseros*. Every year, for a couple of weeks in August, grapes are laid out to dry here to produce the *Pasos Malagueños* — raisins from Malaga that you see in boxes in supermarkets. The grapes are turned frequently to ensure thorough drying and are covered overnight to protect them from early morning dew. For the rest of the year these *paseros* lie fallow.

Just before a crest (30.5km) a *mirador* (📷) at the Km 7 bar and then another (📷) at the Pavo Real restaurant (32.5km ✕) offer extensive panoramic views of the surrounding sierras. Climb for a while and, as you approach Cómpeta, dominated by the tall chimney of its old sugar mill, *ignore* the first roads leading into the village. Drive round the village and then take the road which is also signposted to Canillas de Albaida. **Cómpeta★** (39km ♝▲▲✕M) is worth a short visit, perhaps taking in the wine museum, but don't attempt to drive beyond its main car park; the streets are more suited to donkeys and carts than cars. From here continue round the slopes on the M112, still climbing gently, to the charming and well kept **Canillas de Albaida** (41.6km). Just a few metres past the village entry sign, fork right uphill on a little road signposted 'Acampada' (campsite). It takes you to the 17th-century church of Santa Ana (42km ♝), built on a site which originally held a 9th-century Moorish shrine. Though it looks a bit crumbly, Santa Ana is whitewashed and still in use. Walk 12 starts here and goes to Fábrica de la Luz and over the hills. Perhaps you have time for Short walk 12-1 which leads to a delightful picnic spot by the *fábrica* (**P**12). After looking at the attractive church, take a peep over the sheer drops to the valley behind it.

Leave Canillas the way you came and wind back around the slopes and through the lower part of Cómpeta. When you reach the main road again (45.5km), carry straight on for Algarrobo. Pass a petrol station (46.5km ⛽) and, as you round the valley, again catch sight of Maroma, looking quite benign and belying its 2065m of altitude. Turn right towards Archez (49km) and, now on the descent, you will see several more villages and *paseros*. Cross the substantial bridge over the Río Algarrobo y Sayalonga (51.8km) and immediately turn right on the MA158 signposted to Salares. This road is wide enough to have a central white line!

The slopes are more barren now, but vines still survive among the olives. Maroma is now straight ahead of you, as the road runs down into **Salares** (58km ♔), the sleepy and picturesque village shown on pages 14 and 15. Take a stroll through its steep streets and seek out the 13th/14th-century square minaret which is now incorporated into the church. Continue up the road and on towards Sedella, perched on the slopes of the Sierra de Tejeda, with Maroma as backdrop. Pass the turn into Sedella (60.6km ♔▲▲✗) and continue down the road, signposted to Canillas de Aceituno. The road runs beneath Sedella, passing its hostal/restaurant as you leave the village behind. After negotiating more twists and turns, not far beyond the 'Termino Municipal de Canillas' sign you come to La Rajihe, a delightful picnic/camping area laid out on the slopes amongst tall pines (66.8km ⊼PCT3a).

Snake carefully through the very narrow streets of **Canillas de Aceituno** (69km), admiring its colourful balconies and gardens, then look out for the huge Embalse de Viñuela in the valley below. Follow the long and winding road downhill and, after passing a restaurant (76.8km ✗), turn right on the C335 (77.4km). You are now travelling in a northerly direction and, after passing a cafe/bar (✗) on the left and crossing the Río Bermuza, Viñuela comes into sight over to the left (79.7km ▲▲✗). Notice the enormous U-shaped pass in the mountains ahead: it's the Boquete de Zafarraya, shown opposite. Walk 13 descends through this pass and ends at **Puente Don Manuel** (83km ▲▲✗), a major junction with several restaurants.

Turn left across the bridge and then left again at the junction with the A335, signposted to Vélez Málaga. Very soon (84.3km), following a *hotel* sign, go left once more towards Viñuela; then, almost immediately, turn very sharp right under a bridge. The road winds gently round towards the hotel, perched on a hill and commanding magnificent views across the Embalse de Viñuela to the all-encompassing mountains. You should treat yourself to these views, so park somewhere on the wide track which starts at a stand of cypress trees and runs up the side of the hotel's boundary wall (85.6km). Walk up the track and, as it bears right, the *embalse* is just a few metres in front of

Fuente at Espino, with the El Boquete de Zafarraya behind it (Walk 13)

you. A minor track, which eventually disappears into the reservoir, leads along the bank to a ruined *cortijo* (**P**CT3b).

Then drive on past the hotel, with a further view of the *embalse* as the road runs just above it. Fork right and, back at the A335 (87km), turn right to Vélez Málaga. This good road descends rapidly, leaving the mountains behind and levelling out as it approaches the coastal plain (95km). It narrows on the outskirts of **Vélez Málaga** (98.6km ✚🏔 ✗🚪), capital of the Axarquía. This town dates back to prehistoric times; it has seen the passage of many civilisations, taking the best from each to create the architecturally impressive and cultural centre that exists today.

From Vélez Málaga follow the A335 (sometimes signposted for Málaga and Almería) round the western edge of the town and turn right at the end of the ring road. (The *autovía* will eventually be extended to pass along this stretch of coast so in the future you may have to pass under or over it.) Enter the busy **Torre del Mar** (104km ✚🏔✗🚪 ⊕) and follow signs for Almería along the coast. The N340 is sorry contrast to the quiet attractive roads through the mountains; a ribbon of development runs along both sides with scarcely a break. At least some of the old strategic watchtowers still survive; access to them was by rope or ladder to the top! Carry on past **Torrox Costa** (116km 🏔 ✗🚪), a village which boasts Roman remains, and **Nerja** (124km ✚🏔✗🚪⊕), to reach the turn-off left back to your starting point at the Cueva de Nerja (128km).

4 NATURAL PARKS AND THE GRAND OLD TOWN OF ANTEQUERA

Torremolinos • Parque Natural Torcal de Antequera • Antequera • Colmenar • Parque Natural Montes de Málaga • Málaga • Torremolinos
172km/107mi; 4h-5h driving
On route: ⌘ at Aguas del Torcal, Torrijos; Picnics (see **P** symbol and pages 9-13): 14a-c, CT4; Walk 14

The towering rock sculptures of the Parque Natural Torcal de Antequera, created by the action of rain and wind on soft limestone, almost defy belief and are no less captivating than the grand and often ornate architecture of Antequera itself. In complete contrast, the Parque Natural Montes de Málaga is an area of deep gorges, gentle little valleys and shady woodland — a botanist's paradise. Situated only about 15km from the coast, but rising to an altitude of over 1000m, the mountains of this sierra protect Málaga from the worst weather conditions and provide excellent walking opportunities.

Start from the Aquapark on the outskirts of Torremolinos. Turn left towards Málaga on the access road parallel to the N340. Turn left (0.4km) close to the Ecoahorra supermarket and pass the Palacio de Congresos. Then turn right onto the *autovía* (1.4km), following signs for Málaga.

Ignore exits and skirt around Málaga on what is called the *ronda* (ring road), looking out to the beckoning sierras. Go through an underpass into an area of low hills and follow signposting for Antequera, which direct you off the *ronda* (18km) and onto the N331. Pass a petrol station (20km ⛽) followed almost immediately by signs to a *pantano* (reservoir) and botanic garden — a visit another day.

The road runs alongside the Río Guadalmedina and crosses it frequently. This river was responsible for frequent catastrophic floods in Málaga up until the beginning of the 20th century. The hills bear only a sparse covering of trees, and old and new *cortijos* tucked into the slopes look isolated and exposed. After going through two short tunnels (33km), take Exit 148 (37km) for Colmenar and Casabermeja. If you wished to shorten this tour by 75km, and visit the magnificent Torcal park and the town of Antequera another day, you could turn right and right again for Colmenar now, rejoining the main tour at the 111.5km-point.

The main tour turns left into **Casabermeja** and follows clear signposting for Villanueva de la Concepción and Torcal through the village and out past a major interchange. This delightful road through rolling fields and healthy orchards takes you up through **Villanueva** (53km), a village stretched out along the foot of the barren mass of the Torcal. Pass a *fuente* (57km) and turn left off the road (59.4km), to enter the **Parque Natural Torcal de Ante-**

quera★. Drive uphill past a *mirador* (📷) to the main car park and visitor centre (63.2km; closed 14.00-16.00). Park safely before trying to take in the astonishing sights that greet you. On the right, before the building, is the start of the 1.8km-long walking trail shown on page 13, the 'Ruta Verde' (*P*CT4). Take care to follow the green markers as they lead you between the huge natural rock sculptures, and be aware that vipers and scorpions inhabit some of the nooks and crannies.

When you leave this natural 'museum' of rock, drive back to the road and turn left for Antequera (67km). The road drops steeply, sometimes in hairpin bends, through an area known as the Boca de Asno (Donkey's Mouth) and passes alongside the attractive Area Recreativa Aguas del Torcal (🍴), set out along a pretty canal with shallow falls and inviting pools. Pass the motorable track to it (74.5km) and continue alongside the canal past several well-sited restaurants (✕) to **Antequera★** (79km ✚🛏️▲▲✕🚰⊕), an attractive town dominated by its castle. Driving through the town, always follow signs for Málaga, but *do* park for a while, if only to admire the amazing — sometimes gloriously ornate — architecture of the grand old buildings.

Once out of Antequera go straight on at a roundabout (85km) and then turn right, to get onto the *autovía* (86.5km and ▲▲🚰 at 96km). Leave the *autovía* at Exit 147 (108km) for Casabermeja and Colmenar. Fork left and then right for Colmenar, then go straight ahead at the next junction (111.5km). Still in rural countryside, follow the N356 before turning right on the old MA435 (118km) and right again at the T-junction on the outskirts of **Colmenar** (119km ✚▲▲✕). This friendly village, popular with Malagueñans for weekend lunches, is to the left but the tour follows the C345, heading south. Formerly the main route between Madrid and Málaga, this road is quite picturesque. Be prepared for a spectacular overview of Maroma (2065m) and the surrounding sierras as the road climbs to the Venta de Pinar corner of the densely wooded Parque Natural Montes de Málaga (125km ✕). At another *venta* (✕), ignore a branch of the C345 that goes off to the left (to Comáres, a village perched on top of a hill and visible for miles around). If you stop here to look at the monument to the chief engineer of the *parque* project, don't be surprised if the air is a trifle chilly. The highest point on this stretch is 1031m, over 3000ft.

The main public entrance to the **Parque Natural Montes de Málaga★** is clearly signposted at 132.6km, between the km544 and 545 road markers. Turn down the steep road which takes you to a car park and information board at the Torrijos recreation area (134km ⋤△M). The Torrijos house in front of you, dating back to 1843, is now a museum of old implements, and the whole extensive area is nicely laid out around the fresh-running Arroyo de Chaperas with picnic benches, a camping site and walking trails. Walks 14a and 14b both start here and pass several beautiful and secluded picnic spots (*P*14), one of which is shown on page 100. Take a break from driving and perhaps try one of the short walks mentioned on page 101.

From the park return uphill to the road and turn right. Almost immediately you go through a pass at 900m, the Puerto de León, with a fine coastal view (137km). Just a little further on, at another entrance to the park, you'll find the Fuente de la Reina, a fancy fountain with adjacent bar/restaurant. Walk 14b passes close to this point. As you descend, two 'unofficial' *miradors* (138km, 139.6km 📷) enable you to contemplate the surrounding landscape — there are breathtaking views into the valleys, across to the coast and over row upon row of sierras. At 143km the road drops quickly, looping into the first of two corkscrew turns and tunneling under itself. Beyond the second corkscrew you emerge at an 'official' *mirador* (📷): the views are very fine, but not a patch on those you enjoyed from higher up!

Pass the most southerly park entrance (146km) and continue heading towards Málaga. Cross the ring road (151km) and wind down into the outskirts of the city, to traffic lights. If you wish, continue straight into **Málaga** (✝🏔✕⊕🍴△M), but the main tour turns right, following signposting for Ronda Este and Almería. Wind back uphill and through a tunnel, to join the N340 *autovía* (155km). You are going east — the opposite direction to where you want to go — but this is the *only* access in the vicinity. So leave the *autovía* at the next exit (signposted to Limonar; 155.5km). Turn left for Algeciras and then get back on the Ronda Sur going west. With the Sierra de Mijas prominent on the the right, follow Algeciras signs as far as Exit 228 for Torremolinos, Palacio de Congresos (176km). Leave the *ronda* there and, just beyond the Palacio de Congresos, turn right to the Aquapark (177km).

5 SIERRA DE MIJAS

Benalmádena Costa • Mijas • Puerto de los Pescadores • Fuengirola • Benalmádena Costa

55km/34mi; 1h30min driving

On route: Picnic (see **P** symbol and pages 9-13): 15; Walks 15, 16

Despite being short and never far from the coast, this tour introduces you to an impressive mountain ridge, fertile river valleys and a typically picturesque Andalusian village. There are several opportunities for short strolls or longer walks which will better acquaint you with the country-side. The tour can be accessed from anywhere along the coast, picking it up at its 6km point on the autovía at Exit 223.

Start in Benalmádena on the N340 at the Puerto Deportivo roundabout with the tall stylised sail. From here one road leads down to the Puerto Marina, but you head west along the N340 towards Fuengirola and Marbella. The road runs along the coast passing many hotels, the most prominent of which is the high-rise Hotel Riviera. Just beyond the rather tasteless, red-painted Castillo de Bil Bil, one of Benalmádena's tourist attractions, turn right at a roundabout (1.7km) for Arroyo de la Miel and Pueblo Benalmádena. This palm-lined avenue heads towards the Sierra de Mijas, alongside the Arroyo de la Miel whose waters create a narrow fertile valley on the left. Drive through **Pueblo Benalmádena** (3km ▲▲ ✕) following the *autovía* signs. After a few turns and a couple of round-abouts, with the Tivoli World funfare in between, follow Algeciras signs onto the *autovía* (6km), heading west. But leave the motorway again at the next exit (11.2km) and turn right towards Mijas (11.8km 🚰).

It's a nasty shock coming so suddenly on to this fairly typical country road — narrow, steep and bumpy. With the thickly-wooded slopes of the Sierra de Mijas rising above you, it's a case of peaks, pines and potholes! Over to the left, beyond the scattered villas, the concentrated mass of white houses clinging to the slopes is the pretty village of Mijas. Wind round to it, passing a small, old aqueduct on the left (15.5km) and a succession of en-trances to some grand villas.

At a roundabout, the tour turns up to the right, following signposting to Coín, but **Mijas★** (17km 🚰 ▲▲ ✕ 🚰 ⊕ 🖼 M) is just to the left and you may wish to potter around before continuing. Walk 15 starts in the main square at Mijas and after passing the amazing villa shown on page 104, tra-verses the eponymous sierra — exploring several points of interest, both man-made and natural.

The road to Coín, lined with tall eucalyptus trees, runs above Mijas and passes (17.7km) the zigzag trail up to the

Ermita del Calvario — our first objective on Walk 15 and a delightful picnic site with glorious views (**P**15). It's worth parking at the *mirador* just a little further along the road and making the pilgrimage up to the *ermita* past the stations of the cross. Then, instead of returning down the same path, you could follow Short walk 15 back to the road just beyond your car. From the *mirador* there is a panoramic view over Mijas. Notice particularly the bullring and the amphitheatre which you may not have noticed just strolling through the village.

Continuing along this attractive road, you pass below a large water reservoir on top of a hill. Tucked in just beneath it is the *perrera*, the municipal dog pound (20km). Walk 15 comes down off the slopes opposite this point and heads back to Mijas. Rounding a bend (22km) the green and fertile Entrerrios valley comes into sight, with the peaks of the Sierra Blanca as the backdrop. This is the valley through which the Río Alaminos and the Río de Ojén flow before uniting to form the wide Río Fuengirola.

The Alhaurín Golf and Country Club (23.5km) is overlooked by a strange tower perched on top of a hill. It's interesting enough to warrant closer inspection, so drive on to the roundabout (25.7km) at **Puerto de los Pescadores** and go straight ahead, signposted to Coín. A little way

Typical in all Andalusian pueblos blancos *in the autumn is the wrought-iron balcony hung with* pimientos *(red peppers) set out to dry.*

along on the right, park at the start of a chained access road and make your way up one of the steep paths which take you directly to the tower. It was built in the late 1980s as a 'feature', when the surrounding area was earmarked for more golf-related development. But plans lapsed, and it now stands as an empty shell. Walk all round it, taking in the magnificent 360-degree views. To the west is the Sierra de las Nieves, dominated by Torrecilla (1919m) and, further round to the right, are the twin peaks of Prieta (1521m).

Go back to the roundabout and turn right, heading south towards Fuengirola. Drive through orange groves and rolling grassy hills and notice the *alcornoques*, cork oak trees, on the left (30.6km). Over to the right, on the distant slopes, look carefully, and you will spot the Minas de Talco (talc mines), close to the furthest point of Walk 16. As you descend a little into a heavily-wooded valley, the coast comes into sight. Citrus groves and lush vegetation grow along the valley of the Río Alaminos (34.8km) and, a little further on, is one of the valuable avocado plantations that the area supports. The tour goes straight ahead at the Entrerrios junction (35.6km), but Walk 16, which follows the river up to the talc mines, starts about 3.5km down the road to the right.

Carrying on towards the coast (40km 🎥) and following the Río Fuengirola, the Sierra de Mijas becomes ever more prominent, and the Castillo de Sohayl stands sentinel on a mound on the outskirts of **Fuengirola** (🛏▲✕🎥⊕Δ). If you wish to sample the delights of this typical coastal resort, go straight ahead at a roundabout (41.4km). But to continue the tour, turn left onto the *autovía* towards Málaga. *(NB: at the time of writing, Málaga was incorrectly signposted to the right at this point!)*

Take the next exit Exit 212, signposted to Benalmádena Costa (43.6km) and rejoin the N340. Up on a hill, a *torre* and a *toro* compete for your attention, looking disdainfully down on unattractive tower blocks. Pass through several small resorts and, at the first roundabout (51km), go straight on into Benalmádena Costa. Follow the road all the way past the Mijas turn-off you took on the outward journey and back to the Puerto Deportivo roundabout (55km).

6 SIERRA DE LAS NIEVES

Marbella • San Pedro • Ronda • El Burgo • Guaro • Monda • Ojén • Marbella

150km/93mi; about 4h driving; Detour: 31km/19mi; 45min

On route: ⌁ at Llanos del Plano, Quejigales; Picnics (see **P** symbol and pages 9-13): 17, 19a-b, CT6a-b; Walks 17-20

This tour takes you to Ronda, steeped in centuries of history, and to some of the other pueblos blancos (white villages) of Andalucía. But essentially it is a circuit of the Parque Natural Sierra de las Nieves. This vast expanse of outstanding natural beauty is crossed by high sierras and narrow deep gorges which support a great wealth of flora and fauna. From your car you will see fantastic scenery, but to do the area justice you should take advantage of the many opportunities to leave your car and explore inside the park. To make the most of the trip, choose a day which is forecast clear and sunny and set off early. (Remember, however, that it can be quite chilly at high altitude, even when the sun is shining.) If you wish, this tour can be picked up on the autovía at the 0.3km-point (the Plaza de Toros exit) or the 12km-point (the Ronda exit) and can be combined with Car tour 7, which is a circuit from Ronda.

From the roundabout at the Plaza de Toros take the Ojén road towards the hills. Walk 17 starts a kilometre or so up this road and follows an old trail to the Olivar de Juanar, the olive groves of an old aristocratic hunting lodge, now a Hotel Parador. But at the McDonald's roundabout the tour follows Algeciras signs on to the *autovía* heading west (0.3km). Attractively landscaped gardens attached to villas, restaurants, residential complexes and golf courses reach down to the roadside. So drive with care, watching out for vehicles seeking to enter the fast flow of traffic from a stationary position. The road passes through a tunnel in the rock (5.7km) and shortly thereafter (8.5km) you have the opportunity to take the 31km detour described on page 42 — to Istán: take Exit 175, signposted for Istán and Puerto Banús. The latter is a picturesque yachting harbour with Andalusian style apartments, but the detour takes you into the mountains, to the charming village of Istán (Walk 18).

The main tour continues along the *autovía*, crosses the Río Guadiza (11.6km) and, on the outskirts of **San Pedro**, turns right at traffic lights and a roundabout (12km; signposted to Ronda). This winding road heads directly towards the Sierra de las Nieves. It climbs steadily and, if you are behind a heavy vehicle, it could be a slow journey. Just be patient and enjoy the scenery — and be grateful that you are not travelling on the old road, crumbling sections of which can still be seen. Pass La Quinta, the well-known golf course, a petrol station (14km ⛽) and then the village of La Heredia set in cork oak woods.

All the trappings of the coast are left behind as the road

climbs steadily. Pine trees cling precariously to loose rocky slopes on either side and, in March, the large white flowers of the gum cistus plant attract attention. Soon (starting from about 25km) frequently-signposted viewpoints with good parking (☞) offer spectacular panoramas. As the composition of the rock changes abruptly, the reddish colour gives way to light grey, and the slopes become stark and barren (40km). A statue in contemporary style signals the highest point on the road (44km; 1125m ☞), at the start of a small plateau. At the 136km road marker, a dirt road goes off right (47km) at the western entrance to the Quejigales area of the **Parque Natural Sierra de las Nieves★**. Walk 20, which climbs through the *pinsapo* forests shown on pages 6-7 and up to the Peñón de los Enamorados (1780m) starts about 10km along this dirt road (🅿) — but if you follow it for only 2km, you will reach a delightful picnic spot (**P**CT6a) where you can enjoy a stroll.

The tour continues on the main road (▲▲✕ and 🍴 at 49km); go straight on at all road junctions and you will begin to descend gradually. Your first glimpse of the white houses of Ronda comes at about 53km. The old part of the town, dominated by its church, lies to the left (west) of the town, close to the famous Tajo Gorge. Spectacular to look at, this gorge splits the town in two and is the resting place of many unfortunate souls — from the architect of the 18th-century bridge who fell to his death here as he tried to retrieve his hat to the hundreds of prisoners thrown into the depths by an angry mob during the Civil War.

The gradient steepens as you descend to cross a fertile plain, following signs to Sevilla and Ronda Centro. Considering the altitude and the rugged nature of the encircling mountains, the gentleness of the landscape is an unexpected surprise. Cross the Río Guadalevín and reach a major roundabout on the eastern outskirts of **Ronda★** (61km ✝▲▲✕🍴△⊕M). Car tour 7 starts at this roundabout and completes a circuit inside the Parque Natural de la Sierra de Grazalema — vulture country. This tour turns right, towards El Burgo, but first spend some time in Ronda, a fascinating town whose conquest by several different nations is reflected in its present architecture and culture.

From Ronda return to the roundabout and head towards El Burgo. The narrow, rather bumpy road runs parallel to the railway line, and both are spanned by a fine Roman aqueduct (63km) — incomplete, but impressive none the less. After crossing a plain planted with olive and oak trees, the road undulates across open hillsides, gradually climbing to Puerto del Viento, a pass at 1190m (72km 📷).

Descend from the pass enjoying that 'top-of-the-world' feeling always engendered when mountain peaks spread out beneath you. In stark contrast to the Ronda side of the pass, the surrounding slopes here are almost free from trees — including the desolate-looking Sierra de los Merinos ridge directly ahead, traversed by a line of pylons. But it all changes again soon after you negotiate a spectacular narrow defile between high cliffs and pass through the mountains. Wooded slopes overlook the valley of the Río del Burgo and, in autumn, the broadleaved trees bordering the river create a pretty picture (see opposite).

The road descends sharply through pines to the Mirador del Guarda Forestal (81km 📷) where an elevated monument overlooks the route of Walk 19 deep down in the river valley. El Burgo soon comes into sight below, but it's still a long way down. After more twists and turns, a stand of tall eucalyptus trees welcomes you to **El Burgo** (86km ▲✕🖃), which overlooks a picturesque gorge filled with prickly pears. Drive straight through, following signs to Málaga and noticing the impressive Sierra de Prieta rising on the left. At the far end of the village, cross the bridge over the Río del Burgo. Just below the bridge is the starting point for Walk 19. You'll have to follow the entire walk to reach the beautiful setting shown on page 122, but its two short versions start here as well: Short walk 1 leads to the setting shown opposite (*P*19a), and Short walk 2 visits a charming *ermita* at the Fuensanta *zona recreativa* (⛲🍽️△ *P*19b). A little further on, a track going off to the right (88km) also leads to Fuensanta, which is about 3km away.

The road zigzags out of the fertile plain, goes through the Puerto de las Abejas (820m) and descends through olive groves to **Yunquera** (94km ▮▲✕). The prominent old Arabic watchtower here, the Torre Vigía, is being restored and set up as an information centre for the park. Following signs to Málaga, leave the village behind and pass through a stone arch (the Puente Palo), which used to carry an aqueduct. For as far as the eye can see, almost every inch of land has been cultivated, with citrus trees on the level stretches overlooked by olives on the terraced slopes. The sierras ahead, magnificent at any time, are at their best when silhouetted against the setting winter sun.

Once again, parts of the tortuous old road are a reminder of times past, when mules rather than vehicles passed this way. Even now, mules would perhaps be more appropriate for the steep road you pass (99km) going down to the tiny picturesque hamlet of Jorox, tucked into the hillside and surrounded by citrus orchards.

Wind down past the Granja Escuela (Farm School) and at the **Alozaina** junction (104km ▲▲✕🅿) go right for Málaga and Coín. Eucalyptus trees again grow close to the road as you descend through the still intensely-cultivated countryside. Cross the Río Grande, its grassy banks lined with giant reeds and lush green vegetation, and pass the right turn to Tolox, the main eastern entrance to the natural park (109km ▲▲). Follow the Río Grande past villas and restaurants (✕) with colourful gardens and cross the Río Seco, which carries quite a quantity of water after rain. Veer right, climbing away from the river, and take the right turn towards Guaro at the 57km road marker (118km).

Bypass Guaro (123km ✝▲▲✕), self-styled 'Paraíso de los Almendros' (Almond Paradise) — a name best appreciated at the beginning of the year when this whole valley is resplendent in pink and white blossom. Continue on towards Monda. This village soon appears ahead, dominated by a hill on which the meagre remains of its old castle are dwarfed by a modern luxury hotel. The road circles the hill and takes you through the outskirts of **Monda** (127km ✝🛏▲▲✕M). Pass the *lavadero* (wash-house) and *fuente* on the right and almost immediately turn right for Ojén and Marbella. Pass a track on the right signposted to the Refugio de Juanar (129km) and ascend, again following Ojén and Marbella signposting, to join the C337.

You pass a place called Llanos del Plano (133km 🅰) and then a road to the Refugio de Juanar. Just beyond the Puerto de Ojén (580m), leave the main road: turn off left (134.5km) for a visit to Ojén. Descend into the green valley of the Río de Ojén, where thick vegetation conceals any sign of its old iron, copper, nickel and lead mines. The coast comes into sight before you enter **Ojén★** (138km 🅿✕), a typical Andalusian white village in which the friendly locals maintain old customs and traditions. Drive above the

Picnic 19a: autumnal colours paint a vivid canvas at the first dam on the Río del Burgo.

Landscape on Walk 17, with the peak of Cerro Nicolás in the background.

main part of the village, to the petrol station at the far end. Short walk 17, a delightful hillside ramble, starts and ends here.

Continue up to the main road, following signs for Marbella. As you drive back to the coast, look across the bay. On a clear day, Gibraltar stands out prominently and to its left the Rif, the hills of North Africa, are discernible in the distance. Continue down to your starting point at the Plaza de Toros roundabout (150km).

Detour to Istán

From the 8.5km-point of the tour take Exit 175 to Istán (*ignore the previous exit, 178, also signposted to Istán:* the lack of follow-up signs will leave you going round in circles). Once off the *autovía*, go right and right again (signposted for Istán). You drive up the side of the Los Naranjos golf course. The road runs back parallel to the motorway, before going right at a roundabout (2.1km), crossing the Río Verde and turning left at another roundabout. *(If Istán signs seem a bit confusing, follow Racquet Club signs.)* Once on the narrow winding road heading north there are no deviations; it runs high above the exceptionally lush valley of the aptly-named Río Verde, Green River. The road is being straightened in places, which will slightly decrease the km count.

Pause at the *mirador* (7km 📷) for a view of the Embalse de la Concepción, which collects the water that drains from some of the highest points in the park. Pass the Ermita de San Miguel on the right (12.5km ✝) and come into **Istán★** (15.5km ✝ ▲ ✕), set high above the northern tip of the *embalse*. At the entrance to the village, fork right uphill, to the parking area (being a typical *pueblo blanco*, its streets are narrow, so explore on foot). Walk 18, which starts from the car park, provides a feast for the eyes in the southern part of the park. If you don't have time for even the short version today, at least take a few minutes to stroll out to the *mirador* on the western edge of the village. To get there, walk through the car park and out the far end. Follow the road past the *fuente* and *lavadero* to the church square. Go round to the left, past the church, and follow Calle Río down to the cemetery entrance, flanked by two cypress trees. Turn left past allotments and orchards, then fork right uphill on an attractive little esplanade lined with palm trees. Just beyond the last building, a rocky promontory to the left has been transformed into a tranquil place from where, in the mornings and evenings, the village elders contemplate the wonders of nature (**P**CT6b).

42

7 SIERRA DE GRAZALEMA

Ronda • Villaluenga del Rosario • Benaocaz • Ubrique • El Bosque • Benamahoma • Puerto del Boyar • Grazalema • Ronda

122km; 3h30min-4h driving

On route: ⊼ at Las Covezuelas, Los Cañitos, Los Llanos del Campo; Picnics (see *P* symbol and pages 9-13): 21-23; Walks 21-23

Actually a massif comprising about 16 different sierras, the Sierra de Grazalema has its own microclimate which occasions the highest rainfall in Spain. Botanically speaking it is a wonderland of variety and colour, while its mountains, valleys and rivers provide magnificent walking country. Vultures breed here, and the whole area to the north of the road joining Benamahoma to Grazalema is protected. You must have authorisation to walk there, and from January to June (the nesting season), you must walk accompanied by a guide. This tour, which can be linked with Car tour 6, is a clockwise circuit inside the Parque Natural de la Sierra de Grazalema. Whether you are climbing through high passes or driving through charming pueblos blancos (white villages), look for the vultures soaring and circling above. Those in a large group are likely to be griffon vultures, while solitary birds may be black vultures. With a wingspan of almost three metres (nine feet), they present quite a sight!

Start from the main roundabout on the eastern outskirts of Ronda, following Sevilla signs on the C339, the Ronda bypass. Immediately crossing a steeply-inclined railway line, wind down into a fertile agricultural plain and cross the Río Guadalcobacín (7.5km). Pass the turn off for Setenil, a village whose streets are set into the rocks. Its name is said to derive from the words meaning 'seven nil', in recognition of the fact that the Christians failed seven times to take it from the Moors. Climb gently out of the plain between wooded slopes, ignoring the turn to Montejaque (15km) and taking the next turn-off (16km), the A372 signposted to Grazalema. At 17.7km you pass your return route from Grazalema and continue straight on through a pass, the Puerto de Montejaque.

With the Sierra Margarita ahead to the left, drive down between cultivated fields to the Embalse de Zahara, overlooked by the remains of Zahara castle. From now on keep your eyes open for vultures, but don't forget to pay attention to your driving as well.

Just before the bridge at the southern tip of the reservoir, turn left (25km; signposted to Grazalema). This narrow bumpy road carries few vehicles but, in the summer, you will often see little owls perched on the posts along the verge, behaving for all the world as if they were traffic wardens. Surrounded by craggy hills and wooded slopes, the road winds through an amazingly beautiful valley, where a few *cortijos* rely mainly on olives to provide a meagre living. Whatever the time of year, there will always be colour, whether the reds and golds of the autumn trees, the white of the snow-capped peaks, or the delightful and varied hues of wildflowers and shrubs.

Beyond the Ermita de Nuestra Señora del Rosario (31km), as the gradient increases, a few hairpin bends take you up through an area of holm oaks to a crest from where Grazalema can be seen tucked into the slopes ahead. You will pass through the village later so, at the T-junction (34km), turn left, following signs for Ronda and Ubrique. Wind downhill and cross the Río Guadalete, with the impressive Sierra del Caillo across the valley to the left. Pass a left turn to Ronda (your return route) and start descending, with rocky hills and steep cliffs to the right and open meadows where cattle graze to the left. In summer woodchat shrike perch on overhead cables.

You pass Las Covezuelas, a shady haven with a *fuente* (44km 🛏△), before emerging from the woods to gorse-covered slopes and a cultivated valley which leads to **Villa-luenga del Rosario** (46.5km), the highest village in the province of Cádiz. With cliffs to either side, drive down the aptly named Manga (Sleeve) de Villaluenga, a spectacularly narrow valley. Look out for blue rock thrushes that are attracted by the dry stone dyke that snakes all the way through this valley and stop to admire the views from the attractive Mirador del Cintillo Aguas Nuevas (50.6km 📷), with information panel, benches and a panoramic photograph naming all the surrounding sierras.

Wind down below the *mirador* and, immediately after a *fuente,* turn right on a little slip road to **Benaocaz** (52km ✚▲✕), an ancient settlement created by the Moors in the 7th century and still retaining many old traditions. Walk 22, a glorious trek through the mountains (photograph page 135), starts from the village and offers a variety of shorter options, one of which leads to the river (*P*22). Drive along the narrow streets, some with crazy paving, and when you are faced with a No Entry sign ahead, turn down very steeply to the left. Turn left at the junction by the church and then go right, back onto the main road.

As you pass a leather factory and a junction (59km), Ubrique (✚▲✕🖵⊕), a substantial but not particularly noteworthy town, is just off to the left. The tour turns right, following signposting for Villamartín. Within about 1km you will begin to see, through a gap over to the right, the Salto del Cabrero (Goatherd's Leap), a gigantic cleft caused by a geological fault. This is one of the highlights on Walk 22 and one of its short versions. Don't forget to keep

Grazalema: once a focus of the wool trade, the village now has a reputation for handicrafts and culinary delights.

looking out for vultures as you descend sharply to cross the Río Tavizna, near a new villa development (63km △).

Turn right at a junction for Grazalema and Benamahoma (67km). Some of the place names around here are relics of the Arabic past, with the prefix 'Ben' having the same connotation as the Scottish 'Mac'. At 69km another park recreation zone, Los Cañitos (⊼), lies just on the outskirts of **El Bosque** (▲▲⚔△), a cool and beautiful village with a trout hatchery, botanical garden and visitor centre. Walk 23 comes here from Benamahoma by way of the delightful riverside path shown overleaf. The tour runs along the edge of the village and turns right (70km), following signposting for Benamahoma. Pleasantly shaded with a variety of trees, including eucalyptus, the road passes the track to a launching site for hang-gliders (73km). The Sierra del Pinar, where the *pinsapo* still survives, rises spectacularly ahead. You pass the left turn to Benamahoma (75km ⚔△), which also boasts a trout hatchery and where Walk 23 begins (**P**23). Wind up steeply round some hairpin bends, taking in the views back down over the Benamahoma valley.

Pass a park information panel showing a waymarked 2.5km path to the summit of Albarracín (77km) and then a *fuente* on the left, beside a weeping willow tree (unusual in this part of the world). Beyond **Los Llanos del Campo** (78km ⊼△), continue climbing past some laybys (📷) — one with an information board detailing a short walk to Cerro de la Mesa (Table Mountain). Just after the km42 road marker, there is an official viewpoint with a *fuente*, from where you can see the Salto del Cabrero again. Can

Río El Bosque, not far beyond the setting for Picnic 23.

you spot any of the vultures that regularly patrol the cliffs on the left? Beyond the **Puerto del Boyar** (1103m; 85km) you come to a stone picnic shelter *(merendero; **P**21)* a little further down the road. With the Río Guadalete rising close by, it's a good spot to pause and have a stroll. Walk 21 (photograph page 129) heads into the mountains from here, while Walk 22 comes up from Benaocaz and returns via the Salto del Cabrero.

Continuing the tour, begin a steep descent below craggy rock formations overlooking thickly wooded slopes. On coming to a junction (87km) ignore the left fork to Zahara and Algodonales, two villages at the top end of the reservoir; go right towards Grazalema. Cross the Río Guadalete once more; Walk 21 leaves the road here on its way to the *merendero*. As it descends from the Llano de las Presillas, Walk 21 crosses our route — at Camping Tajo Rodillo (88km △). Follow signposting straight on to the centre of **Grazalema★** (89km ⊹▲✕⊞). The road runs above the village then winds down through the main street, where you can park. Then continue past the petrol station on the outskirts of the village. At the junction with your outward route (91km), carry straight on to the Puerto de Los Alamillos (822m; 94km), where you turn left for Ronda.

The surrounding slopes are again heavily wooded, mainly with cork oaks, and you pass strips of bark sitting in piles at a small cork factory on the right (103km). Leaving the woods behind, keep following signs for Ronda, going right at a junction (104.5km) and then right again on the A376 (106km). Follow Ronda and San Pedro signs back to the roundabout where you started (122km).

☀ Walking

Spain is the second most mountainous country of Europe, with some ranges extending almost to the coast. Many visitors content themselves with admiring the mountains from their loungers by the hotel pool, but that is no substitute for being out there among them. The car tours take you closer, but it is only on the walks that you can enjoy the complete countryside experience. Andalucía is particularly well endowed with nature's blessings and you will delight in the beauty and variety of its flora and fauna. At almost any time of year flowers and trees provide a kaleidoscope of colour. The Nature notes on pages 6-7 explain a little about the interesting things you will encounter most frequently on the walks. ***There is something here for everyone***, with the short walks well within the capabilities of most people, even if the main walks are too long or strenuous.

A few of the walks are linear or 'out-and-back', but the majority are circular, this being not only more practical but also more satisfying. In order to complete circuits, we have sometimes had to include stretches on asphalt roads. But these are always quiet country roads, and you are unlikely to meet any traffic on them. However, do remember that roads and tracks leading to official picnic sites will be crowded and noisy on Sundays and *fiesta*s, when the local people like to have a day out.

It would be unusual while walking if you did not see another soul all day. Even in the more remote areas you will come across goatherds, as well as farmers tending their groves and terraces. Strolling the highways and byways is also a favourite pastime among the villagers themselves. All the people you meet will appreciate a greeting, so say *Hola* (Hello), *Buenos días* (Good morning) or *Buenas tardes* (Good afternoon) when you meet the local people.

It is important that all walkers, whether beginners or experts, read and *heed* the country code on pages 7-8.

G rading and timing

Grading walks is a tricky business. People who can walk all day on the flat without tiring may find even short uphill sections very strenuous. Others who experience no problems on prolonged climbs might nevertheless feel that a three-hour walk is quite long enough. At the start of each walk description we have tried to give a good indication of what to expect, but *if you read the entire walk description* before setting off, you will have an even better picture. Some walks are very long, and others involve steep inclines, going through tunnels, wading in rivers or scrambling on rocky mountain slopes. Be sure to choose walks that are within your capability, remembering that *enjoyment* is the primary aim.

You need not be an expert or even a habitual walker to be able to tackle most of the walks, but a reasonable level of fitness and stamina, as well as some mountain 'sense' , is assumed. The given **timings** do not include any lengthy stops for things like picnicking, extensive birdwatching, plant identification or photography. Allow for these when arranging your outing, and also take account of the weather. Hot sun, driving rain, and strong winds can affect your rate of progress. Check the walking notes frequently to avoid missing turn-offs or landmarks. After testing one or two walks, you will be able to adjust the timings to suit your own pace.

Waymarking and maps

Navigation in the mountains of Andalucía is relatively straightforward, and on the one or two occasions where confusion could occur we have made the walk instructions as clear and comprehensive as possible. A few of the walks follow sections of well-established routes and you will come across a variety of **waymarkers**. There are the red- and white-striped markings of the GR (*Gran Recorrido*) long distance footpaths and the yellow and white of the PR (*Pequeño Recorrido*) short distance walks. Elsewhere there may be coloured dots or arrows, marker posts, or cairns — or a combination of all of these. However, *our walks do not rely on waymarks and, indeed, some can be quite deceptive. It is wise to* **follow our written instructions** *at all times.*

There is considerable discrepancy between commercial **maps** of the area, both walking and military, and the actual situation on the ground. The maps specially drawn for this book were correct at time of writing but, as more of the countryside is exploited, new tracks or roads may appear. All the tracks and paths followed in our walks are overprinted in green, and we would advise you to keep to these. In a region of deep gorges, sheer cliffs and high peaks, it is not sensible to strike off into the unknown.

Where to stay

There are so many **holiday resorts** dotted all the way along Andalucía's coastal strip that you are spoiled for choice. Our walks are spread over a huge area, so wherever you are based, *some* of them will be easily accessible. If you are visiting Andalucía mainly to walk, you might prefer to stay in the mountains. Granada and Ronda have a range of **hotels**, and in other towns and villages there are *pensiones* and *hostales*. There are well equipped **campsites** in most regions, too. Tourist offices provide a list of accommodation, but it is by no means complete — village bars are a better source of information and advice.

Getting about

The coastal strip and main routes inland are quite well served with **buses**, but elsewhere timetables are designed to suit the local population rather than walkers. But it *is* possible to make use of buses for some of our walks and we have included the relevant timetables (see pages 141-142). They may vary according to season, so always check times before setting off. It is also worthwhile remembering that buses have a habit of passing intermediate places on their route much earlier than expected. In the villages, the bars or *tabacaleras* in the main square can usually tell you when buses run through, but do take their advice with a pinch of salt unless you see a written timetable. Note that not all tourist offices hold information about buses.

For some of the walks you could make use of a **taxi**, agreeing the fare in advance, or arrange to stay overnight close to the area where the walk starts.

But, undoubtedly, the best way of getting to the walks described in this book is by **car**. Hire one through your travel agent when arranging your holiday or book direct with a hire company. Prices are very reasonable in spring and autumn, which of course are the best seasons for walking. You *can* hire locally, but it is often more expensive and less easy to solve problems, should any arise.

Weather

The mountains of southern Spain protect the coast from the worst weather conditions and contribute to the climate which makes it so popular as a holiday destination. Undoubtedly the best seasons for walking are spring and autumn, when temperatures are comfortable and the countryside is at its colourful best. In the heat of summer, attempt only the shorter walks, or those graded 'easy' —

but, even then, be cautious in the sunshine. And avoid high level walks in winter, when the ground can be snow-covered for several months.

Because this book covers such a large area, it is impossible to generalise about the weather; indeed, with the large variation in altitude on some of the walks, you might experience all four seasons in one day. Fierce storms can occur unexpectedly at almost any time of year, so make

Walk 1: descending the old trail (Carrigüelas)

sure you are prepared. The strength of the sun should never be ignored, and it can be blisteringly hot from June to September. Temperatures in the mountains can be extreme, falling as low as –15°C and rising to over 40°C.

In the Sierra Nevada and the Alpujarra, the main rains tend to come in autumn. The Sierra de las Nieves and the Sierra de Grazalema are wettest from December to February, the latter range having the highest recorded rainfall in Spain. Much of the rain is torrential and falls in short periods of time, so there are usually plenty of dry sunny days. Of course the rain falls as snow in the mountains.

Always take account of prevailing conditions, remembering that a warm sunny day can turn bitterly cold with the passage of just a few clouds. Obtain local forecasts if possible. We have found these to be quite reliable, with Radio Gibraltar being particularly useful for walks 17-23.

What to take

The time of year and prevailing weather conditions will largely dictate what you should carry with you. But things can change rapidly in the mountains and with even the lowest sierras rising to over 1000m, it is best to equip yourself for all eventualities on all the walks.

For sun protection, take **suncream, sunhat** and **long-sleeved shirt**. For the mountains, take **warm** and **waterproof clothing**. The whole area tends to be very rocky underfoot, so wear **stout, thick-soled shoes, preferably with ankle support.** Unless you are walking in extremely bad weather or in snow, you should not require heavy boots, but for comfort we certainly recommend proper lightweight hiking boots. Be prepared for paths and tracks to be muddy for a day or so after heavy rain. The other essential is **water**. Various mineral waters are available in different-sized bottles in all grocery shops and supermarkets in the area. There are *fuentes* on many of the walks, but in summer months you may find they are dry (and in the Alpujarra the water often tastes bitter). For all longer walks you should take a **picnic lunch**. Where necessary, we specify extra items you will require.

All the walks can be followed without a **compass**, but it would be foolish to tackle any of the high mountain ones without one. Mist or cloud can soon obliterate landmarks and lead to disorientation. For **emergencies**, it is always wise to carry a **first-aid kit**, some high energy food, extra water, a couple of large black plastic bags, whistle, torch and additional warm clothing.

Potential hazards

Dogs present little threat in this region of Spain. The fiercer ones are chained up or fenced in, while those left to run loose, though noisy, lively and curious, are harmless. But *do* carry a 'Dog Dazer' if dogs worry you; these are now available from Sunflower Books.

We have seen neither **snakes** nor **scorpions** on our walks in Andalucía, but they *do* exist — so be careful when walking through scrub, and don't disturb rocks and stones. A huge variety of **mushrooms** appear in damp areas, particularly in autumn. Some are likely to be highly poisonous, so don't be tempted to pick, or even touch, any of them.

Deep gorges should also be treated with care and caution. Invariably the cause of accidents is carelessness and a breach of the rules of common sense.

Organisation of the walks

The walks chosen for this book represent the best walking areas within the vast Andalusian region. We have divided them into seven groups, stretching from the Almuñécar area (Sierra Nevada and Alpujarra), through Nerja/Torre del Mar (Sierra de Almijara), Málaga (Montes de Málaga), Torremolinos/Fuengirola (Sierra de Mijas) to Marbella (Sierra de las Nieves and Grazalema). *Wherever you are staying, there will be easily accessible one-day walks.*

Begin by taking a look at the fold-out touring map and locating those which are nearest to you. The route notes and detailed map will give you an idea of what to expect, while the photographs are intended to whet your appetite. Every itinerary begins with planning information — distance, grade, how to get there, what to take, and the total ascent of the walk. This should tell you whether the walk is within your capabilities — an ascent of 750m/2500ft is pretty tough! Wherever possible, we suggest shorter walks and alternatives, when the main walk is strenuous.

The **maps (all 1:50,000)** have been specially annotated for use with the text and feature the following symbols:

▬▬▬	main road	540	spot height	●	snow pit *(nevera)*
———	secondary road	🚐	bus stop	↗	spring.tank, etc
═══	motorable track	🚗	car parking	∩ ■	cave.building
▬▬	other track	📷	best views	⌂	rock formation
- - - -	footpath	⚲	church.chapel	⌐	information panel
— —	river.stream	†	shrine.cross	⛏	hydroelectric plant
-·-·-	*acequia*	■△	castle.camping	⚒∩	factory. aqueduct
<u>3►</u>	main walk	☼⚒	mill.quarry	❀☗	garden.monument
<u>3►</u>	variation	🏛	picnic tables	P	picnic (see page 9)

1 BUSQUISTAR • BAÑOS DE PANJUILA • FERREIROLA • ATALBEITAR • PORTUGOS • BUSQUISTAR

See also photograph page 50   **Distance:** 13km/8mi; 3h58min

Grade: moderate-strenuous with ascents and corresponding descents of 480m/1575ft overall — a few of them steep, but none prolonged. You must be sure-footed and have a head for heights. *Note:* a landslide in autumn 1997 destroyed a small part of the main walk path, near the 2h18min-point. It is now repaired but, if the problem recurs, you will have to follow the Alternative walk back to Busquístar, missing out the three villages.

Equipment: see page 51; *walking boots are essential.*

How to get there and return: 🚗 to/from Busquístar (the 81km-point on Car tour 1); park in the picturesque church square.

Short walk: Río Trevélez (2km/1.2mi; 44min). Easy, with descent and corresponding ascent of just 150m/500ft; equipment as on page 51; access as main walk. Follow the main walk to the 20min-point by the river and the mill and return the same way.

Alternative walk: Baños de Panjuila (9.5km/5.9mi; 2h51min). Moderate, with ascents and corresponding descents of 420m/1380ft, some of them steep; equipment and access as main walk. Follow the main walk to the 2h05min-point. Take the path which rises in short zigzags, eventually reaching a LEVEL PATH (2h23min). Turn right and, with Busquístar visible ahead and fantastic views of the valley below, climb gradually, passing a white post under a huge precarious-looking overhang. The path descends from here to cross a TRACK (2h31min), continuing through trees and above terraces, undulating gently towards the village. An earthen path takes you across a bridge, and you begin the steep climb to the FIRST OF THE HOUSES (2h48min), where walls and balconies are festooned with flowers or, in autumn, *pimientos* (photograph page 36). Wind up through the village to CHURCH SQUARE (2h51min).

This is probably as enjoyable and satisfying a walk as any we have ever done. With a starting point at 1160m, you are already in the heart of the mountains, and the high peaks will often be covered in snow. The landscape varies from gentle to rugged as you traverse the ancient paths and trails. Life in the little villages and *cortijos* along the route seems hardly to have changed in hundreds of years, and the accepted mode of transport is still the horse or donkey. Although a fantastic walk at any time, it is particularly enjoyable in spring, when the wildflowers are at their colourful best, and snow still lingers on the mountain tops.

Start out from the CHURCH SQUARE with its *fuente*, bar and weeping willow tree. From the *mirador* overlooking the lower terraces, glance across to the hills on the far side of the valley, where some of the paths you will follow are visible. Then wind down the pretty concrete path at the side of the Bar Vargas — overlooking some typical Andalusian flat roofs. As you leave the village behind, turn left through a gap in some railings. A steep earthen path takes

53

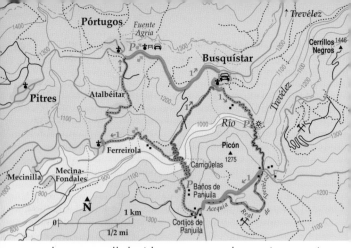

you between tall deciduous trees and terracing, passing above a BUILDING (**10min**) which has recently replaced an old *cortijo*. It levels out a little above cultivated plots, then steepens again and zigzags downhill, leaving the terracing behind. The distant sound of the water in the Río Trevélez filters up from below as the path becomes rocky and, by the time you reach the river, at an old GRAIN MILL and a BRIDGE (**20min** *P*1a), the noise can be quite thunderous.

Make a short detour to the left, just before the bridge, on a path which covers a disused *acequia*. It leads to an old dam where large fish swim in pools of clear fresh water. Return and cross the bridge (**28min**), then zigzag steeply up the trail on the far side. Pause and look back at the dam, at Busquístar and at the evergreen oaks that cling precariously to the hillside. The trail is substantial, and one feels quite secure despite the sheer drops into the valley. It is still used regularly by locals with their donkeys, and mint, sage and thyme grow in profusion all the way up.

At **50min** reach the brow and then skirt almost level around the hillside. Opencast iron mines can be seen across the *barranco* on the left and, in spring, the slopes are resplendent with broom and lavender. A gradual climb brings you to an always-bustling *cortijo* set on the corner at a ROAD JUNCTION on the route of Car tour 1 (**59min**). Up on the left are some old abandoned buildings, probably associated with the mines. Here you can either turn right (signposted to Torviscón) and walk up this quiet road for a short distance towards the Cortijos de Panjuila, or cross over and descend to a path which runs roughly parallel to the road, alongside the old **Acequia Real de Trevélez**. The path rejoins the road about 200m before the Cortijos. In the valley on the left, beyond the groves of almonds, olives and figs, are the ruins of an old mercury mine. Listen for stonechats, warblers and rock sparrows which enjoy the solitude here and delight in flowering almond blossom.

Fork right to the **Cortijos de Panjuila** (**1h21min**) and go up the track past the little white cottages, no longer permanently inhabited. Look out for the ravens which often soar above the hill ahead. Leave the main track which continues round the base of the hill, and take the initially-grassy track going downhill past NO 4, THE LAST COTTAGE on the right. Enjoy the company of the lively small birds and be prepared to flush some noisy partridge. At **1h34min** you reach the mineral spring and ruins of **Baños de Panjuila** (**P**1b). On the left, a little way past the ruins, is a tiny stone bridge which takes you to a *fuente*. Beyond the bridge some rocks above the old bathing pools provide a superb place to pause. On the slopes on the opposite side of the valley are perched eight little Andalusian villages, startlingly-white against the hillside. You will visit three of them before returning to Busquístar.

As the route, a bit overgrown and muddy at the outset, continues beyond the *baños,* stop and look across the valley. You will be able to see the route of the Alternative walk snaking directly up the rocky slopes in short zigzags.

But for now, continue on to the medieval trail shown on page 50, the **Carrigüelas** — an amazing feat of engineering, with the steep slopes carefully stepped to ease the gradient. As the trail zigzags steeply down towards the river, you'll see the pipes and buildings of a disused hydro-electric plant *(fábrica de la luz)* and another old mill which still contains a few relics of its working past. Cross the BRIDGE over the river (**2h03min**) and continue on the trail, bearing left past the MILL. The trail starts to climb across some slaty rocks and, almost immediately, the zigzag path you saw from above goes off to the right (**2h05min**). *(The Alternative walk follows this zigzag path.)* The main walk continues straight on. Notice the old terraces across the river, where grain was grown for processing in the mills. The rocks are alive with wheatears and, in spring, you will be entertained by the musical song of serins.

As you pass along the top of terracing, you have your first views of Ferreirola and Pitres ahead. All the villages around here are connected by an amazing network of paths, and this walk samples only a few of them. Continue climbing gradually and, at the point where some RUINS lie just below the path, *ignore* a red-waymarked path up to the right (it eventually connects with the Alternative walk). When the trail opens out a little, cross an open expanse of

This pretty fuente, *decorated with old tiles, is reached at about 2h33min, not far outside Ferreirola.*

rock, bear right into deciduous woods then cross a small BRIDGE over a stream (**2h15min**). If you have problems with a landslip beyond this point, retrace your steps and take the zigzag path of the Alternative walk. Otherwise, continue past a fine example of an *era* (threshing floor) on the left; it looks just like a balcony, with views over a little house and a *barranco* (**2h30min**).

When you reach the *fuente* shown above, be warned that the water has a high mineral content — tasting a bit like soda water. And though the tiles *are* genuinely old, we were told by a man we met there that they were added quite recently by an Italian friend of his. Proceed up the slope and through **Ferreirola** (**2h41min**). During the time of the Arabs, this tiny village became one of the most important places in the Alpujarra because of its silk production and its four springs.

Just before the *lavadero* and the *fuente* at the entrance to the church square, turn right up a steep little road. Immediately on the left, a notice advertises rooms, Spanish courses and walks. The road becomes a charming, flower-lined trail which takes you up to the foot of the village of **Atalbéitar**. Just below the first house, take a narrow path to the right, along a grassy terrace. It soon turns upwards and meets a wider PATH (**3h05min**) on which you turn right and follow the GR7 signs towards Pórtugos.

This is a steep trail, often brilliantly yellow with gorse and, in autumn, carpeted with chestnuts that have fallen from mature shady trees. It's not long before Pórtugos can be seen high above. Continue climbing, then turn left on a wide TRACK (**3h13min**). On reaching a PYLON (**3h25min**), the track forks. **Pórtugos** is just off to the left, but take the right fork, which leads to the ROAD. Turn right and start descending gradually, reaching the *ermita* at **Fuente Agria** within a few minutes. The water here is bitter (see notes on pages 18-19), but it is a pretty spot well laid out with picnic benches by the stream (**P**1c). As you continue down the pleasant and mostly tree-lined road, you can look over to the ground covered on the first part of the walk. Walk along the top of **Busquístar** and round to your car (**3h58min**).

2 CAPILEIRA: THE THREE BRIDGES

Distance: 5km/3mi; 2h30min

Grade: moderate, with ascents and corresponding descents of 340m/ 1120ft overall, including quite a steep climb at the end.

Equipment: see page 51.

How to get there and return: 🚌 to/from Capileira (the 67km-point on Car tour 1); park where you can in the centre of the village and make your way down to the Vista Veleta apartments (see plan of Capileira on the touring map).

At an altitude of around 1435m/4700ft, Capileira is an excellent starting point for walks into the Alpujarra. Recent efforts to take advantage of this have resulted in a network of colour-coded waymarked trails and a series of information panels throughout the area. But their maps are rather difficult to follow, and the colours and arrows on the wooden waymarking posts are often confusing. We have used them merely as *landmarks* where appropriate, rather than direction indicators.

This delightful walk up the Poqueira Valley, mostly on old trails, takes in the three bridges which lie below Capileira. Draining from the high peaks of the Sierra Nevada, the river is always clear and fast-flowing, and the abundance of water makes it possible to exploit to the full the fertility of the surrounding countryside, much of it steeply sloping. Market gardens and cultivated terraces produce a

Goatherd and his flock encountered at about 1h25min into the walk, between the first and second bridges

variety of crops and fruit trees. In spring, herbs and delicate wildflowers line the paths, while in autumn, the huge spreading chestnut trees provide the splendour and the shade, and the crunch of nuts underfoot.

Start out at the **Vista Veleta** apartment block: walk to the right of it and continue downhill below Calle Alamo, noticing the village *mirador* off to the right. Take the steep and sometimes messy track at the edge of the village, heading downhill past houses with animal pens on the ground floors. At the foot of the village, take the path which starts beside an INFORMATION PANEL (**6min**) and winds round to the left below the village.

Heading towards Bubión and Pampaneira, descend around fenced cultivations, where horse and plough are still regularly used, and meet a STREAM (**25min**) which always seems to be overflowing. The path levels out and turns to the right, where there is a *cortijo* guarded by three dogs. (You can face down the loose one, which is noisy and fierce-looking, but harmless.) Wind left past the *cortijo* (**39min**) and zigzag past some ruins, to a track. Turn right and reach the valley floor close to the first of the day's bridges, **Puente del Molino** (**43min**).

Cross the bridge and climb straight up the far side, through trees. Bear right, away from a tiny footbridge across a stream, and look up, to where you can just make out the lowest houses of Capileira on the opposite slopes. On coming to the corner of a fence, go up to the right of a little HOUSE (**54min**), climbing through shrubs, flowers, grasses and herbs. Pass a WAYMARKING POST (**1h**) as you climb steeply and pass a fine example of an *era,* as the pleasantly shady path bears right and contours the slopes, all the while heading upriver. Cross a stream and *ignore* a waymarking post directing you up to the left. Instead, go right, across another stream, and almost immediately reach a FORK (**1h15min**). Both routes lead to the same place, so take your pick and soon pass another WAYMARKING POST (**1h20min**). The path becomes overgrown in parts as it contours above two *cortijos*, the second in ruins. Again faced with a choice of paths, take either of them and pass below a *cortijo,* to meet another path at a T-JUNCTION (**1h 33min**). Turn right and descend to the river at the second bridge, the **Puente Chiscar** (**1h39min**).

Cross this bridge and head uphill on a path which crosses a small *barranco* (**1h43min**). Almost immediately, fork left across the *barranco* again and head upriver to join another path (the outward route of Walk 3), just before a

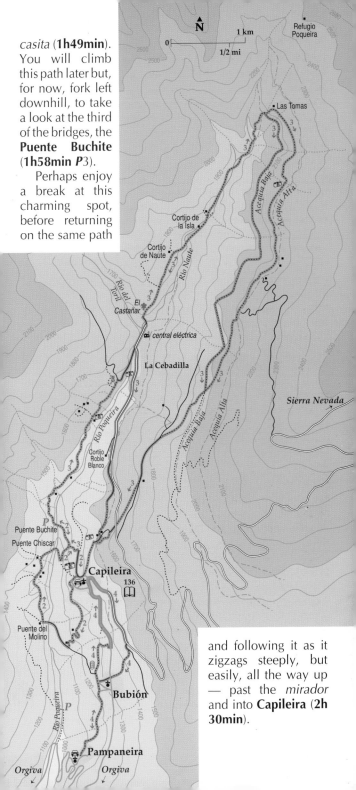

casita (**1h49min**). You will climb this path later but, for now, fork left downhill, to take a look at the third of the bridges, the **Puente Buchite** (**1h58min** *P*3).

Perhaps enjoy a break at this charming spot, before returning on the same path

and following it as it zigzags steeply, but easily, all the way up — past the *mirador* and into **Capileira** (**2h 30min**).

N

0   1 km

1/2 mi

Refugio Poqueira

Las Tomas

Acequia Baja

Acequia Alta

Cortijo de la Isla

Cortijo de Naute

Rio Naute

Rio del Toril

Rio del Toril

El Castañar

central eléctrica

La Cebadilla

Sierra Nevada

Rio Poqueira

Cortijo Roble Blanco

Acequia Baja

Acequia Alta

Puente Buchite

P

Puente Chiscar

Capileira

136

Puente del Molino

Bubión

Rio Poqueira

P

Pampaneira

Orgiva   *Orgiva*

3 RIO NAUTE AND THE MULHACEN APPROACH

Map page 59   **Distance:** 21km/13mi; 6h20min

Grade: strenuous but not difficult, with ascents and corresponding descents of 1000m/3300ft overall. The high altitude may cause shortness of breath, so take it easy on the climbs. Be prepared for wet and muddy patches where water drains off the slopes.

Equipment: See page 51; *walking boots are essential* and take a swimming costume if you wish.

How to get there and return: 🚌 to/from Capileira (the 67km-point on Car tour 1); park where you can in the centre of the village and make your way to the *mirador* (see plan of Capileira on the touring map).

Short walk: Puente Buchite (3km/1.9mi; 56min). Easy, despite the descent and corresponding ascent of 300m/1000ft; equipment as page 51; access as main walk. Follow the main walk for 25min and return the same way.

Shorter walk: La Cebadilla (8km/5mi; 2h38min). Easy-moderate, with ascents and corresponding descents of 320m/1050ft overall; equipment as page 51; access as main walk. Follow the main walk to the BRIDGE (1h38min). Cross it and then pick up the Alternative walk at the 3h16min-point, to return to Capileira (2h38min).

Alternative walk: Cortijo de la Isla (14.5km/9mi; 4h15min). Moderate, with ascents and corresponding descents of 470m/1550ft overall; equipment and access as main walk. Follow the main walk to the **Cortijo de la Isla** (2h25min). After taking a break, climb back up to the *cortijo* with the *era* and retrace your steps downriver to the NOTICE PANELS BY THE BRIDGE (3h06min). Cross this and the next two bridges and follow the dirt road that runs below **La Cebadilla** (3h16min). It becomes surfaced and climbs gradually. Ignore a track to the right (to Cortijo Roble Blanco; 3h33min); take the next track to the right (at a WAYMARKING POST; 3h38min). Level at first, this track follows an *acequia* which you will see below. Soon the track narrows into a path and passes a couple of *cortijos*. It eventually rises, crosses the *acequia* (encased in a pipe at this point) and brings you to a restored *cortijo* with a high wall (3h51min). Turn right on the track by an INFORMATION PANEL AND POST. Then fork right off the track (3h59min) on a path that descends past a little WATER CONTROL HUT. Now pick up the main walk at the 6h04min-point, to reach Capileira (4h15min).

This excellent walk, full of variety and a naturalist's delight, takes you all the way up the valleys of the Río Poqueira and Río Naute until you are just under the skirts of Mulhacén (3482m/11,420ft), the highest point on the Iberian Peninsula. On your return route, at an altitude of almost 2200m/7200ft, the Veleta ridge seems only a stone's throw away. Always magnificent, these mountains of the Sierra Nevada are dazzlingly beautiful when the sun shines on the lingering snow.

Since this is a long walk, try to set off early, so that you can enjoy a leisurely break at Cortijo de la Isla beside the Río Naute — an idyllic spot, with fine views of Mulhacén. Early birds will also be more likely to catch a view of the *cabra montés*. The ibex (see photograph page 2) roams the western slopes and likes a morning drink from the river.

Don't worry when you find yourself going in the *opposite* direction to most of the waymarking on the first part of the route; see our introductory paragraph for Walk 2.

Starting from the *mirador,* take the track which passes to the right of the INFORMATION PANELS. It follows the Poqueira River upstream and, at a WAYMARKING POST (**11min**), winds down to the left on a steep, but stepped, wide and rocky path. You descend to another WAYMARKING POST (**16min**), where Walk 2 comes in from the left and joins this route. Fork right along a level path which passes a stone *casita* and then descends to the river at the **Puente Buchite** (**25min** *P*3), where the Short walk turns back. Cross the BRIDGE and head right, continuing the trek upriver. This path, narrow at times, leads up to and round an *era* and old *cortijo* (**38min**), where it levels out for a while. Towering over the head of the valley, Mulhacén comes into view for the first — but by no means the last — time. Also visible are the white houses of La Cebadilla upriver on the opposite bank.

A steep ascent takes you to another *cortijo* (**50min**), where we were once lucky enough to see, crossing our path just ahead, a herd of about a dozen *cabra montés*, making for the seclusion of nearby trees. There are several more *cortijos* along the route, in various stages of repair. Most are long-abandoned but, as your path passes along the top of some fields, you will realise that the whitewashed farm ahead is a working *cortijo*. As you get closer (**1h08min**), its noisy but harmless dogs will probably run up to greet you. Just beyond the farm, at another POST, head down to the right, through a bank of shady willows. Cross a STREAM where, in mid-October, broom still flowers among the red autumn berries. At a fork, choose either path and head above RUINED ANIMAL SHELTERS and on to another STREAM (**1h18min**). When you reach an *era* at another *cortijo* (**1h20min**), it's worth pausing to take in the views back down the valley.

At a WAYMARKED JUNCTION go straight ahead towards a pylon. This area is well cultivated, providing great feeding for small birds; look especially for redstart and larks. Reach the PYLON (**1h25min**), built on an *era*. From here you can see a dirt track below; carry on to where the path meets it at another post (**1h28min**) or take a short-cut straight down to it. Turn right on the TRACK and soon, as you round a bend, the views up the valley to Mulhacén are breathtaking.

On the opposite bank is La Cebadilla, a little hamlet built to house the workers at the hydroelectric plant further upriver. Continue to a BRIDGE (**1h38min**) and turn left before crossing it. *(The Shorter walk crosses over to* **La Cebadilla**.*)* Now on a narrow concrete road, cross the next bridge at the HYDROELECTRIC PLANT, the point where the Río del Toril and the Río Naute unite to form the **Río Poqueira** (**1h41min**). Follow the dirt track which continues up the Naute, crosses another bridge and leads to an information panel and multicoloured WAYMARKING POST (**1h45min**). Take the path which rises to the right of the INFORMATION PANEL and winds high above the bridge through **El Castañar**, a chestnut grove. The route up the stepped rocks is not difficult, but take it slowly, remembering the altitude. Pass another WAYMARKING POST (**1h54min**) and enjoy intermittent views of the many waterfalls that cascade down the cliffs opposite. You can regain your breath as the path levels off and heads around a rocky tree-covered mound, before heading upriver again.

Ignore the WAYMARKED ROUTE up to the left (**2h11min**) and continue above the white, isolated but inhabited **Cortijo de Naute**. After the next WAYMARKING POST (**2h16min**) turn down right at yet another *cortijo*, also with an *era*, and start the short descent to the river. When you reach the water, continue upriver and across a little stone BRIDGE, to some ruined stone shelters and a grassy *era*, part of the

Cortijo de la Isla (2h25min). *(The Alternative walk turns back here.)*

From here you will continue up the valley but, first, take the opportunity to linger here; it's the sort of place one usually only dreams about. Set between the clear, fast-flowing river and a lazy stream surrounded by shady trees, you could not wish for more. Yet there *is* more. There is Mulhacén watching over the valley. Enjoy a picnic and perhaps a dip, remembering that although the water may be icy cold, the sun is strong at 1700m (almost 5600ft). Isolated as the area is, we can't guarantee that you will be alone up here. Once, just as we were preparing to leave, we were joined by a family group with two horses, panniers heavily laden with chestnuts. A young boy on the back of one horse seemed quite happy facing its tail!

When you are ready to continue, take the rocky path that runs upstream and winds up to a WAYMARKING POST **(2h30min)**. From here there is good YELLOW WAYMARKING as far as the 5h53min-point. Your next target is the *cortijo* you can see directly ahead, high on the slopes of Mulhacén. Cross the river on a stone BRIDGE and continue up the opposite bank past the ruins of the main part of Cortijo de la Isla. Go left at a fork, passing a POST at the top of a rise **(2h46min)**. As the valley narrows, cross the river again and

wind up past another POST **(3h)**. Water tumbles and gushes all around and, if you look across to the right, you may see icicles dripping from an overhang just before some waterfalls.

The river splits again and, after a steep rise to TWO POSTS, the path crosses a tributary, making use of convenient rocks, and reaches the MAIN RIVER **(3h13min)**, which comes straight off

The Veleta ridge, from the Acequia Alta (about 4h20min into the walk)

Mulhacén. Winding higher, the path passes another WAY-MARKING POST (**3h25min**); at this point you'll hear the Naute (sometimes referred to as the Río Mulhacén on this stretch), raging through the ravine below. At a LARGE REDDISH BOULDER, a post directs you to the right. But you will avoid what could be a tricky water crossing if you walk to the *left* of the boulder and rise to the Acequia Baja, where a narrow path takes you alongside the canal and round to two more WAYMARKING POSTS (**3h30min**). This *acequia,* the lower of a pair, runs down either side of the valley. Because it is fed from the waters that run off the slopes here, this area is known as Las Tomas (The Takings).

(*Detour route:* If you have really had enough climbing, you can now avoid any more by following the *acequia* (photograph opposite). Reed-lined and about a metre wide, with a narrow path running along the valley side, it winds in and out of the mountain folds. Vertigo is a slight possibility in places and, although we had no problem crossing the many small waterfalls during a dry spell in March, it could be different after heavy rain. It's a lovely walk but it will take about 15 minutes longer than the route over the top — and also deprive you of the extraordinary views from the higher path. But you *will* have an excellent view back to the *cortijo* and the *refugio* above Las Tomas, tucked in under the summit of Mulhacén. And as you round the last deep and narrow ravine, you'll see a working farm below. Just past this point, you come to a WAYMARKING POST, where the main walk crosses the *acequia*. Pick up the main walk at the 5h05min-point.)

The main walk continues from Las Tomas, following the WAYMARKING ARROW uphill, to pass to the right of the *cortijo* you saw from below (2120m; **3h35min**). Within a few minutes, a WAYMARKING POST with a yellow circle directs you downhill.* From here, the path descends and continues along a level stretch. Mesmerised by the grandeur of the Veleta ridge, you may miss the next couple of POSTS (**3h49min**, **3h59min**). But keep your eyes open beyond them, as you cross a waterfall: we saw an alpine accentor in this spot. The path winds up to cross a windswept, grassy slope. As the path undulates past some RUINS AND A POST (**4h06min**), you'll see the Acequia Baja and some of the

---

*A tall signpost a few metres higher up points to the Refugio Poqueira — a substantial mountain refuge which is about half an hour's walk away, on the slopes directly above the *cortijo*. Sitting at 2500m, with a capacity of 87 and every facility a mountaineer could possibly need, including a telephone, it is always open and usually manned.

On the Acequia Baja (the detour route), with Mulhacén rising in the background

old *cortijos* it used to serve on slopes below you.

After the next POST (**4h 17min**) and a final climb, you come to the **Acequia Alta**, the upper of the two watercourses. At 2190m/7200ft, this is the highest point of the walk. Pause for a moment to savour the views shown on pages 62-63 before continuing. The path runs just below the *acequia* but comes right alongside it as it passes below a *cortijo* at the next POST (**4h29min**). Descend to a *casita* and another POST (**4h39min**) and ignore a track going up left to the Sierra Nevada road.

As you proceed now, you will be able to see your outward route snaking along the far side of the valley — and appreciate just how much ground you have covered. It's all downhill from here! You pass a POST (**4h56min**) and then wind down to the Acequia Baja, where there is another POST (**5h05min**). (This is where those who declined to 'take the high road' rejoin the main walk.) Cross the *acequia* and continue the descent. You cross a water pipe (**5h25min**) and enter the pine woods you've been gradually approaching (by another POST; **5h29min**).

Follow the steep path down a firebreak, then go left on a forest track (**5h35min**; POST). Beyond a WATER CONTROL BUILDING, head off right (POST) on a path down the left-hand side of another firebreak. This brings you on to a forestry road at an INFORMATION PANEL (**5h53min**). Cross the road and wind down the TRACK that starts a few metres to the right. As you draw level with a FARM and an enclosure with several notices over to the right (**5h59min**), look left: a POST marks the start of a path.

Follow the path downhill and turn left past a WATER CONTROL HUT (**6h04min**, POST). Pause here to look back and marvel at the 3000m-high ridge that you have been so close to. Then carry on; the *mirador* soon comes into view below, followed by the roofs of Capileira. From another INFORMATION PANEL at the edge of the village (**6h13min**), go steeply right downhill, past a *fuente* and round into the centre of **Capileira** (**6h20min**).

4 THREE ANDALUSIAN VILLAGES:
PAMPANEIRA • BUBION • CAPILEIRA

Map page 59   **Distance:** 8km/5mi; 2h25min

Grade: moderate, with ascent and corresponding descent of 430m/ 1410ft. Some sections are steep and rough underfoot.

Equipment: see page 51.

How to get there and return: 🚌 to/from Pampaneira (the 60km-point on Car tour 1); park in the public car park at the entrance to the village.

Short walk: Bubión (3.5km/2.2mi; 1h03min). Easy, with a gentle ascent and corresponding descent of 240m/790ft. Follow the main walk to Bubión (34min) and return the same way.

This walk links the three most typical of the Andalusian villages. Set in the Poqueira Valley, their curious Moorish-style houses are built one above the other in layers and connected by walkways and a system of *acequias*. And everything is whitewashed — even some of the bells in the church at Capileira! Popular with tourists, each village has its share of cafes, bars and handicraft shops. This walk, mostly on long-established mule trails, presents quite a different perspective, allowing you to appreciate how things might have been in the past. Irrigated by the waters that run off the white peaks of Veleta and Mulhacén, the valley is fertile and supports a huge variety of mature trees. The reds and golds of their autumn hues, as they reflect the sunshine, make this a particularly splendid walk around October.

Start out from the CHURCH in Plaza de la Libertad. Both in 1976 and 1977 Pampaneira won the Spanish equivalent of the 'best-kept village' award, and it remains neat and enchanting today. Take the little cobbled road which climbs uphill between the BAR and a HANDICRAFT SHOP. Turn left off the road, going up the steps past the *lavadero* and a *fuente*. Continue up towards the SUPERMARKET but, just before reaching it, start zigzagging upwards to the top of the village. Here you will find an INFORMATION PANEL and WAYMARKING POST. Follow the BLUE WAYMARKING; it soon directs you to the left, along the rocky terracing which runs above market gardens and past a huge WATER TANK.

Ahead are the villages of Bubión, dominated by its church, and a little higher up, Capileira, with a wonderful backdrop — the high ridge between Veleta (3398m) and Mulhacén (3482m). Skirt the terraces and keep right at the forks, always continuing gradually uphill, enjoying the aroma of the mint which grows along the route. Just after crossing a STREAM (**20min**), there is a fine example on the left of a nicely restored *era*. The path crosses a few more streams; in parts cobbled and stepped, it takes you past the

The church at Pampaneira, seen through the wash-house (lavadero) at the start of the walk

lavadero and into the tiny main square at **Bubión** (**34min**), where you can rest on the low wall in front of the 16th-century church and drink from the fountain.

Bubión's narrow streets form a brilliantly-white labyrinth. Walls and balconies are adorned with colourful pot plants and flowers. Every possible container — buckets, tins, baskets — is used. From here one is quite unaware of the fact that this village advertises itself as a tourist attraction. All evidence of the 'Villa Turística', all the leather work, dried flowers and decorative cloth sold as souvenirs, is confined to the main street at the top of the village. *(From here the Short walk returns along the same path to Pampaneira.)*

Cross the square diagonally to the left and head along the foot of the village, towards the sports complex. Pass to the right of **Casa Mariano** (**38min**) on a path which climbs gently towards Capileira. Chestnuts, cherries, apples and walnuts grow in the market gardens below, with ever-improving views towards Capileira and the Veleta ridge.

This path used to go all the way to Capileira, but in recent times fences, a small landslip and erosion caused by sheep has made it too difficult. So look carefully for a NARROW PATH going back up to the right (**47min**); you may just about be able to discern vestiges of yellow paint marking it. (If you reach the landslip you've missed it.) Follow the narrow path up a steep grassy bank, with a STONE OUTBUILDING to the left and TERRACE WALLS to the right. Meet

Capileira and the Veleta ridge

the TRACK from the building and turn right, winding up to the ROAD (**54min**). Follow the road left towards Capileira, about 1km away (aside from weekends and *fiestas,* the road should not be too busy). You pass the Mirador del Perchal and reach the tourist information kiosk, at a fork in the centre of **Capileira** (**1h09min**). This lively place, the last outpost before the Sierra Nevada, has a little museum dedicated to the customs and traditions of the area.

If you wished, you could catch a bus from here back to Pampaneira, or walk back the same way. But the main walk takes a different route down to Bubión. First you must climb a little way up the road that crosses the mountains to the Sierra Nevada ski centre: fork right and follow the ROAD all the way up through the village, passing the municipal CAR PARK AND PICNIC BENCHES (**1h18min**). Here you leave most of the traffic behind. On a left-hand bend, at the KM5 ROAD MARKER, a makeshift *mirador* (**1h27min**) provides a resting spot for village elders on their habitual twice-daily strolls. Continue to a similar spot a little further uphill, just beneath a line of CABLES (**1h30min**), where a CHAINED-OFF TRACK goes down to the right. You're directly above Bubión — a village of doll's houses under its enormous church.

Turn down the track and look out for a WAYMARKING POST (**1h34min**) at the foot of a path going up to the left: it signals your onward route down to the right. It's a rough, but wide and pleasant path descending steeply through a wood of evergreen oaks. It becomes cobbled on passing the first apartments of the **Villa Turistica** holiday complex (**1h 49min**) and leads to an information panel on the main road through **Bubión** (**1h52min**).

Cross over and head down through the narrow streets, bearing slightly right, to the CHURCH (**1h55min**). Pass to the left of it and retrace your outward route back downhill to **Pampaneira** (**2h25min**).

5 RIO CHICO

See photograph page 17   **Distance:** 8km/5mi; 2h20min

Grade: easy, with ascent and corresponding descent of 320m/1050ft. A little care is needed navigating when you leave Carataunas.

Equipment: see page 51.

How to get there and return: 🚌 to/from Orgiva; park near the old petrol station, just before the bridge across the Río Chico (the 45.4km-point on Car tour 1).

Short walks: both circuits are easy; equipment as main walk.

1 **Bayacas** (4km/2.5mi; 1h23min). A very gentle ascent and corresponding descent of 250m/820ft. Access as main walk. Follow the main walk to **Bayacas** (45min), cross the river, and follow the track downstream and back to your car.

2 **Carataunas** (4km/2.5mi; 56min). A fairly steep, but easy, descent and corresponding ascent of 100m/330ft. Access: park outside the bar at Carataunas junction (6km from Orgiva; the 52km-point on Car tour 1). From the BAR at the junction, walk towards the village. Just before the first buildings there is a large CONCRETE BLOCK at the right hand side of the road. Turn downhill here and follow the main walk from the 1h18min-point to the 1h41min-point. Then turn left up the COBBLED PATH alongside the cables and pick up the main walk at the 50min-point, to climb back to your car.

This delightful river walk takes in two tiny whitewashed villages. The river runs strongly except in summer, when any water that still flows is channelled off in *acequias* and used for irrigation. The result is a very fertile river valley and a haven for birds.

To begin, go up the road at the back of the old PETROL STATION. The road becomes unsurfaced, with smallholdings either side, growing oranges, olives and vegetables. Some of the olive trees are centuries old and provide shade for the more delicate crops planted beneath them. The first of many tall eucalyptus trees lie on the left between you and the river. Beyond the smallholdings, the road becomes a track as it nears the banks of the **Río Chico** (**15min**).

You'll notice several *casitas* clustered together on the opposite bank, one with a solar panel and satellite dish! Leave the track at the point where a house is perched high on a hill on the opposite bank, crossing a RICKETY BRIDGE (**20min**). You will return this way again later, after traversing a figure of eight. On the far side of the bridge, a stony mule trail takes you upriver; there are many places to stop and admire the scenery or picnic by the waterside (*P*5a). The trail continues upstream, sometimes disappearing, sometimes fanning out into a network of small paths. It's never more than about 20m from the water. You will pass one or two *casitas*, and eventually Bayacas appears ahead, the reddish colouring of its solid-looking church and square bell tower contrasting with the whitewashed houses. Turn left when you meet a track which fords the river and walk

69

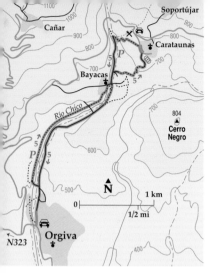

into **Bayacas** (**45min**). It doesn't take long to explore the steep narrow streets of this tiny flower-bound village.

From here cross the river and turn left up the track you followed originally. Directly ahead, on the hillside, you can see a retaining wall: a bar/restaurant is at the left-hand end and Carataunas, your next destination, at the right.

Turn right on an old cobbled trail (**50min**), initially following a line of OVERHEAD CABLES. It climbs gradually and runs below some ruined houses, before turning left and zigzagging up between them. At the top houses the trail deteriorates and, lined with giant reeds, winds round to the left and up onto the hill. After a few more zigzags, you pass the sports ground on the edge of Carataunas and reach the ROAD (**1h18min**). Your return path starts just a few metres to the left, beside a CONCRETE BLOCK. But before continuing, walk right, into **Carataunas**: the church, *fuente,* and tiny Casa Consistorial are worth a visit, and the bar/restaurant is a perfect refreshment spot. The white mulberries that grow around here used to support the worms that, in Arab times, made the village famous for its silk production. The Arabs also exploited nearby deposits of cobalt and nickel.

From the concrete block the path descends to the right. Just before it becomes indistinct (at the point where there is an OLIVE TREE on the left and a WALL on the right), turn downhill. You will hear the Río Chico below. The path zigzags down the terraces, heading generally to the right. If you lose the path, just make your own way down, crossing an *acequia* just before reaching the RIVER (**1h36min**, **P**5b). Turn left on a TRACK. Passing the left turn alongside the line of cables, you complete one loop of the figure of eight (**1h41min**). Continue ahead, to join the track which comes across the ford from Bayacas. Follow it downstream, past a long copse of eucalyptus trees which conceals some little stone cottages. Just beyond the end of the copse, you pass the rickety bridge of your outward journey and the end of the figure of eight. Carry on down the track to the PETROL STATION (**2h20min**).

70

6 CAMINO DE LA ESTRELLA (PATHWAY TO THE STAR)

Distance: 22km/13.6mi; 6h23min

Grade: strenuous — on account of its length. Ascent and corresponding descent of 550m/1800ft, with just one steep section near the start.

Equipment: see page 51.

How to get there and return: 🚌 to/from the Maitena Visitor Centre on the banks of the Río Genil (the 45km-point on Detour 2 of Car tour 2). Alternatively, you can take a better road: turn off the main Sierra Nevada road and go through Güéjar Sierra.

Short walk: Estación de San Juan (4.5km/2.8mi; 1h15min). Easy, with a gentle ascent and corresponding descent of 120m/395ft; equipment and access as main walk. Follow the main walk to the 43min-point, cross the bridge to the Estación de San Juan, and return along the tramway.

This well-maintained, well-used and PR-marked path was originally built to serve the iron and copper mines high up the Genil Valley. La Estrella was just the name of one of the mines, but we really did find this to be a most heavenly walk and the path well named. As if mixed woodland, clear-running streams and colourful flowers and berries were not enough, the magnificent 3000m-high ridge of the Sierra Nevada beckons from the head of the valley. To see it all at its best, choose a clear day and bear in mind that the sun won't be in a suitable position for photographing the high peaks until around 3pm. Being an out-and-back walk, you are not obliged to finish it but, if you do cut it short, make sure you at least go to the Mirador del Genil (1h54min), for views you will never forget.

Start out by crossing the BRIDGE and going through a short TUNNEL, onto the old TRAMWAY. Pass the old **Maitena Station** and go through another short TUNNEL which lies between the Restaurante Los Castaños and Restaurante El Charcón on the opposite side of the Río Genil. Cross the BRIDGE (**13MIN**) to the Café Bar Chiquito and continue, with the river now on your left. Just before the tramway goes over a bridge then through a very short tunnel, little more than an archway, take the clear path, with yellow and white PR WAYMARKINGS, which goes up to the right (**19min**). This is the start of the Camino de la Estrella, which you will follow all the way up the Genil Valley and beyond it.

Rise above the river and cross a stream (where you may see dipper), and pass along the back of a WATER CONTROL BUILDING (**33min**). Cross another stream and go up past ruined alpine-style chalets and along a FENCE (**40min**) surrounding chalets still in use. Wind downhill and cross a WOODEN BRIDGE over the Barranco de San Juan, an excellent picnic site (**43min**; *P*6). The old **Estación de San Juan**, now an occasional café, is to your left on the far side of the Río

71

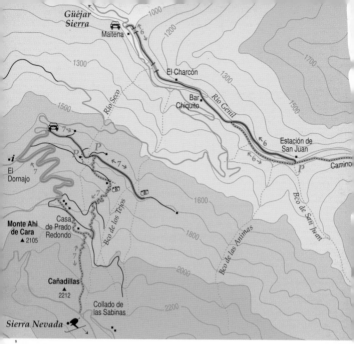

Genil, at the end of the tramway. (*The Short walk crosses to the station here and returns along the tramway.*)

From the *barranco*, go up the slope on a wide path; it continues to follow the Río Genil upstream, winding steeply uphill. After emerging from the trees, the path levels out, then undulates lazily towards the mountains. You will pass the huge chestnut tree shown overleaf; its branches and gnarled contorted trunk and roots overhang the path. Affectionately known as **El Abuelo** (the Grandfather; **1h 18min**), it is said to be the most massive tree in the valley. On the slopes on the far side of the river are the almond groves which used to be tended from the old *cortijo* high on the hill, now in ruins. Red-legged partridge seem to like this area, and we flushed several groups.

Ignore a path going down left to cross the river (**1h 20min**) and another, very faint path (**1h40min**), which climbs to the old *cortijo*. On rounding a bend at a rocky PROMONTORY (**1h45min**), you overlook the confluence of two *barrancos*. But resist the temptation to stop for a break here; continue ahead, passing a clear path down to a semi-cylindrical mountaineering hut on the river bank (popular starting point for an assault on the north face of the Sierra Nevada ridge). Soon after, round a bend, you come to the **Mirador del Genil**, with PR MARKINGS on one of the rocks (**1h54min**). Unsurpassed views of Alcazaba (3366m) and Mulhacén (3482m) make *this* the place to pause.

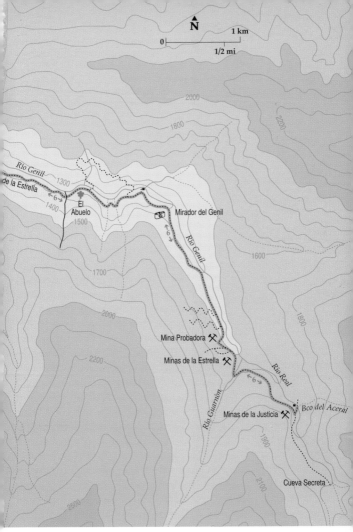

Beyond the *mirador*, the path undulates in the setting shown overleaf, eventually coming to ruins of old houses at the **Mina Probadora (2h31min)**, the best known of the mines in the Sierra Nevada. The mining tunnel still exists today, extending deep into the mountainside. A few slaty steps take you up and across a waterfall, and the path climbs steeply for a while. Take it easy, remembering that you are walking at altitude. A couple of narrow paths come off the mountain from the right, just before a bend where the Veleta ridge appears ahead. Descend to ruins below, the Cortijo and **Minas de la Estrella (2h50min)**, in an open grassy spot where another tunnel remains as evidence of past activity. This site overlooks the confluence of the Río

Stone bridge over the Río Guarnón (top); path beyond the Mirador del Genil, with Mulhacén in the background (middle); El Abuelo, 'grandfather' of chestnut trees (bottom)

Real, which drains Veleta, and the Río Guarnón which drains Alcazaba and Mulhacén. The two unite to form the Genil. Cross the stone bridge over the Guarnón (shown left), before heading up the Real.

The path, now narrower but still clear, climbs to more ruins, the **Minas de la Justicia (3h 18min)**. Just beyond these, take the steep path on the left, down to the the lower mine houses closer to the river. You can reach the water's edge from here, near a NO FISHING NOTICE; (**3h20min**). Although the main path continues for a further half hour or more to Cueva Secreta, another base camp for major climbs to the peaks, our walk ends at this excellent picnic spot, to allow plenty of time for the return.

Go back the same way, past Cortijo de la Estrella (**3h55min**). Then remember to fork down right where the two little paths go up left into the mountains (**4h**). Pass the mine houses (**4h 08min**), the *mirador* (**4h40min**), the path to the hut (**4h46min**), and El Abuelo (**5h18min**). When you reach the **Estación de San Juan (5h48min)**, either return the way you came or cross the bridge to the station building and go back along the tramway. Perhaps stop for a drink and a snack at the Bar Chiquito, before returning to the **Maitena Visitor Centre (6h23min)**.

7 COLLADO DE LAS SABINAS

Map pages 72-73   **Distance:** 7km/4.3mi; 2h30min

Grade: strenuous, given the high altitude — take it easy. Ascent and corresponding descent of 570m/1870ft, including a final steep climb to the Collado de las Sabinas.

Equipment: see page 51.

How to get there and return: 🚗 to/from the 38km-point on Detour 2 of Car tour 2 (not far beyond the Sierra Nevada Visitor Centre); park off the road on the hairpin bend to the left, where a track (waymarked in red) goes off to the right.

Shorter walk: Casa de Prado Redondo (5.5km/3.4mi; 1h47min). Moderate because of the altitude, with an ascent and corresponding descent of 220m/725ft. Equipment and access as above. Follow the main walk to the 56min-point near the Casa de Prado Redondo, then forego the ascent to the *collado*: pick up the main walk again at the 1h39min-point.

Alternative walk: Barranco de los Tejos (5km/3mi; 1h15min). Easy, with a gentle ascent and corresponding descent of 100m/330ft — but be aware of the altitude. Equipment and access as above. Follow the main walk to the WAGON WHEELS (16min), then continue along the track. The mountains at the head of the valley loom larger and the terraces of the Genil Valley come into view just before the track crosses a running stream through the **Barranco de los Tejos** (25min). After passing a chained entrance to orchards on the left, the track runs level across the top of terracing. Just beyond some RUINS on the left (33min), the track is chained (35min). The land ahead is private, but you can continue a little further uphill for closer views of the mountains. When the FARM comes into sight below (39min), take a last look around then retrace your steps back to your car.

Fresh mountain air and the fragrance of pines make this walk an exhilarating experience — with the added attraction of seeing the high peaks of the sierra, snow-covered for about 10 months of the year, in all their glory.

Start out by going down the TRACK (RED WAYMARKING). Almost immediately the 3000m ridge of the Sierra Nevada comes into view ahead. Ignore a track to the left (**3min**) and start climbing. As the track bends right (**8min**), the serrated crags of Alcazaba (3366m) appear, while the lesser crags below the Collado de las Sabinas tower above you to the right. At a JUNCTION (**11min**), take the track furthest to the left, through shady pines (the middle track rises to a cabin, **P**7a). Cross the **Río Seco** and notice the variety of trees that line the route — including oak, juniper and hawthorn. Fork right (**13min**) and soon reach a 'balcony', where two old WAGON WHEELS signal a *finca* just below (**16min**; **P**7b). Just 20m/yds further on, take the path up to the right, SIGNPOSTED to the Collado de las Sabinas. *(But for the Alternative walk, continue along the track.)*

Cross a track (**21min**) and then fork left to pass a ruined *casita*. Go right at a fork (**26min**) and zigzag uphill towards a pine wood under the crags. Pass to the left of the pines (**31min**) and pause to look around. Over to the left, the

The Casa de Prado Redondo, where the Shorter walk turns back

main sierra ridge rises majestically beyond the deep gully formed by the Barranco de los Tejos. Behind you lies the Genil Valley, focal point of Walk 6.

When you meet a track (**41min**), turn right, heading along the crags you saw from below. Above you can see electricity cables and the pointed peak of Monte Ahi de Cara. After walking about 100m along this track, go left on a pleasant path which climbs steadily through low pines. Kestrel hover above, perhaps eyeing the partridge you are likely to flush from the low vegetation. Meet another, somewhat eroded, track (**50min**), turn left and then take the next path to the right (SIGNPOSTED; **53min**). Soon after passing under the cables, reach a JUNCTION with a rocky outcrop ahead. The ruined house shown above, **Casa de Prado Redondo**, is off to the right (**56min**). *(The Shorter walk turns right here.)*

From here take the SIGNPOSTED PATH to the left, through more pines. Soon (**1h04min**) the Barranco de los Tejos is on your left and the barriers on the old Sierra Nevada road — our goal — are visible above. The final climb is quite hard work, and the last section a bit of a scramble, but the views as you breast the **Collado de las Sabinas** (2180m; **1h19min**) make it all worthwhile. You reach the old road at around the KM31 marker, close to a turn-off signposted 'Albergue' (one of a series of hostels along the ridge).

When you have caught your breath, retrace your steps to the last JUNCTION, where the Shorter walk declined the delights of the col (**1h39min**). Go straight ahead, passing behind the **Casa de Prado Redondo**, and continue down the path below the rock face. After a while it becomes a track, running above one of the major tracks you crossed earlier. Adjacent to a CHALET on the right (**1h46min**), take a path going right: the old road comes into view ahead, and you join it just before the KM26 MARKER. There are plenty of short-cuts if you want to avoid the zigzags but, keeping to the road, approach the **Visitor Centre** (**2h24min**) and turn right just before it, to descend to your car (**2h30min**).

8 TOMA DEL CANAL

See photograph page 24   **Distance:** 14km/8.7mi; 4h23min

Grade: moderate, with ascents and corresponding descents of 550m/ 1800ft overall, including some sustained climbing from Toma del Canal. The main and alternative walks should not be attempted just after heavy rainfall, as the Barranco del Buho may be subject to flash floods.

Equipment: see page 51; *walking boots with ankle support essential.*

How to get there and return: 🚗 car to/from the Fuente del Hervidero (the 10km-point on Detour 1 of Car tour 2). You *could* start this walk at the 15min-point (the end of the detour) and save a half an hour's walking. But we like filling up water bottles at the *fuente* before setting off and relaxing with a beer or late lunch at this country restaurant on the return.

Short walk: Puente de los Siete Ojos (5km/3mi; 1h20min). Easy, with ascents and corresponding descents of 170m/560ft overall. Access and equipment as main walk, but trainers will do. Follow the *Alternative walk* to the 40min-point ('Bridge of the Seven Eyes') and return the same way.

Alternative walk: La Cortijuela — Collado de Trevenque — Collado de las Chaquetas (14km/8.7mi; 4h07min). Moderate, with ascents and corresponding descents of 540m/1775ft overall. Access and equipment as main walk. Follow the main walk almost to the 15min-point, but instead of going up on to the raised car park, continue on the narrow GRAVEL ROAD up the Huenes Valley and past a chain barrier designed to keep out unauthorised vehicles. As the valley closes in (34min) ignore the path that goes down to an *acequia* above the river, and reach the **Puente de los Siete Ojos** (Bridge of the Seven Eyes; 40min; *P*8). Follow the road as it crosses the bridge and climbs steadily with just the odd zigzag. A track comes off Cerro Gordo from the left just before **La Cortijuela**, a forestry house (1h36min). This has a charming botanic garden run by the Junta de Andalucía and open at weekends. From here the road swings round to the right and becomes little more than a track. Thus far the terrain has been lightly wooded, but it now thickens as you pass behind Trevenque's triangular peak. At the **Collado del Trevenque** (2h01min) a path goes up the ridge, heading for the summit. Forego that pleasure and continue up to the WATERSHED between the Huenes and Dilar valleys (2h08min). The terrain then opens out as you begin to descend. The Dilar Valley, overlooked by the rugged crags of Los Alayos, is visible below before you round a bend and come upon an open grassy meadow with farm buildings (2h20min), the **Collado de las Chaquetas** — known locally as a goat supermarket. Replenish your water bottles at the *fuente,* then continue on the track which bears right, up towards a pine wood, before starting to descend again. The track sweeps round a hairpin bend to the left as it crosses the bed of the **Barranco de Aguas Blanquillas** (2h33min). Just after the bend, take a wide path off to the right (RED WAYMARKS). You join the main walk at the 2h49min-point. Follow it back to the **Fuente del Hervidero** (4h07min).

Toma del Canal is the point where water is drawn from the Río Dilar and pumped into the Canal de la Espartera. This canal then transports it around the hillsides to a water tank on the slopes of the Boca de la Pesca, only to be dropped back into the Dilar Valley further downstream, to fuel the turbines at the power station (Walk 9). This is an enjoyable walk at any time, but we particularly enjoy it in autumn when the trees are at their colourful best.

Start out by facing the BAR/RESTAURANT. Take the track going right, past a tree and under cables, heading straight towards the rocky triangular peak of Trevenque. On meeting a narrow road, keep left: the road soon becomes unsurfaced as it follows the Huenes Valley. Pass under more cables and go up to the right, past some notice boards and onto a raised area used as a CAR PARK (**15min**).

Across the Dilar Valley are the rugged crags of the Alayos de Dilar and to the right, towering over the old Cortijo Sevilla and a couple of other buildings, is the pointed Boca de la Pesca. You'll be seeing more of this twin-peaked mountain, shown on page 24, later on. Take the path which runs just to the left of the narrow but substantial **Canal de la Espartera** (yellow and white PR WAYMARKS). Notice, too, the upper track marked 'Camino de la Dehesa' — your return route.

The canal, enclosed at this point, alternately appears then disappears underground again. Very soon after joining the canal, you must *leave it* to avoid a landslip (just after a ruined house up on the left). This detour comes up when the canal goes into a TUNNEL with 'windows'. Just beyond the second 'window' (**24min**) take the NARROW PATH down to the right. It descends through low scrub and meets a clear path below. Turn left here and rejoin the

original route beyond the landslip, at the point where it descends below a TELEGRAPH POLE (**38min**).

From here you will undulate pleasantly in and out of trees as the delightful path contours the hillsides. Rounding the tall cliffs that circle the **Barranco del Buho** (**50min**), the sound of water filters up from far below. Further on, from a rocky *mirador* with a PR SIGNPOST (**1h06min**) you'll see a waterfall in the tree-lined Dilar Valley and perhaps witness a golden eagle on the hunt. The path continues gently downhill, and the countryside opens out as you draw closer to the river. After easily negotiating a couple of minor landslips, a dry DITCH crosses your path (**1h20min**). It's too wide to jump, so go down into it and out the other side.

Ascend a little, still through pines, noticing the canal up on the left. Ignore a track down to the river (**1h33min**); your path brings you to the river not long after, at **Toma del Canal** (**1h49min**). Your onward path, PR WAYMARKED, goes left just before the first building, close to a cherry tree and a fig tree. But first you will want to explore this beautiful spot. A narrow path leads a little way along the river to another building where there are more fig trees, and you have a chance to dip your fingers in the icy clear water. The only disturbance is likely to be the squawking of jays.

Continue the walk by going up between rocks, on the

79

path by the first building. It leads behind and then away from the building, crosses the canal and heads steeply up the slopes. Sometimes indistinct and overgrown, the path crosses a JEEP TRACK three times before bearing right and climbing to the flat area above a now-defunct mountain refuge hut, **Cortijo Rosales** (**2h13min**). The surrounding ground, churned up by wild boar, is much appreciated by red-legged partridge.

Take the forestry track which winds steeply up around the *cortijo,* and prepare yourself for breathtaking views. Pass a *fuente* at a new stone MOUNTAIN HUT set in a fantastic spot overlooking the mountains and valley (**2h26min**). The path levels out for a short distance before climbing again to another level area, where the **Barranco de Aguas Blan- quillas**, frozen in winter, goes back to the right. Take the narrow path which rises steeply to the left and, within a few metres, meet another path (**2h49min**). *(The Alternative walk comes in here from the right.)* Turn left and notice the RED PAINT MARKINGS which you will follow for a while.

This undulating path runs above your outward route, so the Dilar River is now far away down on the left. From a crest, the highest point on the walk (1760m/5775ft), you will see ahead the Arenales, sandy-coloured slopes. Head for them (*ignoring* one misleading RED WAYMARK which appears to direct you down a *barranco*). On coming to a sad- dle (**3h10min**), you'll see a jeep track cutting across the hillside straight ahead; you will join it later. Your path is heavily trodden by goats, and you may have to barge through the multicoloured herd as it blocks your way.

If you are lucky you may see a *cabra montés* silhouetted on top of the ridge. You will definitely see the crags of Trevenque up to the right and, below them, to the left, the rock formation they call La Esfinge (The Sphinx). From the saddle the path drops into a wide gravelly *barranco*, the top end of the **Barranco del Buho**. Follow this easy route downhill until you come to a wide signposted path, the **Camino de la Dehesa** (**3h29min**), near a stand of pines. Follow this path to the right, leaving the *barranco*. Just as the path becomes vague, you reach the JEEP TRACK, which runs the length of the backbone of the Trevenque ridge. Cross the track and head downhill, bearing left and then zigzagging between large rocks. Meet the track again and follow it downhill, taking short-cuts. Soon you see ahead the point where you first joined the canal. Survey your out- ward route down to the left, then continue on to the CAR PARK (**4h06min**) and the **Fuente del Hervidero** (**4h23min**).

9 BOCA DE LA PESCA

See map pages 78-79; see also photograph page 24

Distance: 13km/8mi; 5h50min

Grade: strenuous, with ascents and corresponding descents of 740m/ 2430ft overall. You must be sure-footed and have a head for heights. Be prepared for river crossings and be aware of the altitude.

Equipment: see page 51; *additionally: boots with ankle support, compass, towel, extra socks, plenty of water; optional plimsolls for river crossings.*

How to get there and return: 🚗 car to/from the Fuente del Hervidero (the 10km-point on Detour 1 of Car tour 2).

Short walks: equipment as on page 51; access as main walk

1 **Sierra Nevada view** (2.5km/1.6mi; 50min). Easy, with ascent and corresponding descent of 145m/475ft. Follow the main walk to the 25min-point on **Cerro de las Pipas** and return the same way.

2 **Boca de la Pesca summit** (4km/2.5mi; 1h50min). Moderate, with ascent and corresponding descent of 250m/820ft. Follow the main walk to the 58min-point and return the same way.

Alternative walk: Dilar Valley (10km/6.2mi; 4h04min). Strenuous, with ascents and corresponding descents of 640m/2100ft overall. Access and equipment as main walk (less towel and socks). Follow the main walk to the 2h09min-point by the **Río Dilar**. After resting and exploring, return by the same path (it starts between the last ELECTRICITY POST and a CONCRETE BLOCK) as far as the WATER TANK (*cámara de carga*; 3h08min). Cast a last look back into the Dilar Valley and take the path to the left, which skirts the hillside. It soon runs through the trees along the bottom edge of the wood. Follow it across the saddle, round the slopes and under the crags of Cerro de las Pipas. Head downhill (3h45min) through the scrub and fields to the **Fuente del Hervidero**.

At 1522m (almost 5000ft), the aptly-named Boca de la Pesca (Fish-Mouth), is no mean mountain. But although it provides the focal point for this walk, there is much more to enjoy. The upriver trek is delightful at any time of year but, after significant rainfall, when the path at times disappears under water, it becomes an adventure!

Start out with your back to the *fuente* and RESTAURANT. Ahead, locate the distinctive rocky outcrop shown overleaf, Cerro de las Pipas (1428m), your first objective. Cross the Huenes Valley road and go straight ahead through a wheat field; there's no definite track, but you'll see where folk have previously trodden in the clay soil. Cross a track into another field and cut left towards the hillside. Leaving the fields behind, make your way up the slopes through low scrub, herbs and lavender. Head for the right-hand side of the crags, crossing a couple of paths en route. From the crest, not far below the summit of **Cerro de las Pipas** (**25min**), the 3000m ridge of the Sierra Nevada is awe-inspiring. Boca de la Pesca, not as high but nevertheless imposing, is directly ahead, and your onward path is clear, running towards the woods on its northwest face.

After crossing a small saddle, choose the path which

Left: approaching Cerro de las Pipas; right: Alayos de Dilar

you see leading all the way to the edge of the wood, meeting the wood a little more than halfway up the line of trees (**48min**). Follow it up the edge of the wood for a short distance, then turn left and zigzag up through trees. Just below the summit the path meets a FIREBREAK. To the left, you see the top of the manned lighthouse-like fire watch station and on the far side of the firebreak is the path you will later take downhill: having located it, continue to the top, the higher of the twin summits of **Boca de la Pesca** (1522m; **58min**).

From a stretch of low wall you can safely admire the panoramic views. To the left, across the *boca*, is the sharp twin peak with trig point (1514m) and a lone holm oak. Behind it, rising majestically in the distance, is Trevenque (2079m), the dominating peak of this immediate region. Straight ahead, to the southeast, are the Alayos de Dilar, a line of rocky crags overlooking the Dilar Valley. Towering at the head of the valley is Pico Veleta (3398m), second highest peak of the Sierra Nevada. Behind you, the Vega de Granada extends beyond la Zubia and on to Granada itself. From the left-hand end of the wall, locate your next target, the Central Eléctrica de Dilar, a hydroelectric power station far below on the banks of the river.

Once ready for the descent, go back to the other end of the wall and pass between some trees, to join the path you identified on the way up. It will take you all the way to the river. It is very steep and stony and *requires care*. It passes to the right of the *cámara de carga* (**1h18min**), a WATER CONTROL BUILDING where the Canal de la Espartera (Walk

8) ends. From here the water is dropped back into the valley to power the turbines of the *central eléctrica.*

The path crosses the canal just below the building and starts you on the second part of the descent. It's still rough, and stony and steep in places but, if you ignore the almost-vertical short cuts and keep to the longer, gentle zigzags, you'll find the going much easier than on the upper section. Listen and look out for ravens, choughs and crag martins. Soon after passing alongside some retaining walls and crossing a small *barranco* (**1h52min**), you come to a promontory overlooking the setting shown below (right).

Set off again and reach the foot of the path at the DIRT TRACK (**2h09min**) that runs along the river from Dilar, a village 5km to the right. This is a glorious spot to rest and perhaps picnic and explore a little. To the right, picnic benches sit among the trees by the riverside and about 1km further on is a *merendero,* open at weekends. To the left are the power station buildings and some delightful areas close to the water. In the mornings and evenings *cabra montés* come down from the slopes to drink here.

Continuing the main walk, turn left on the track. *(The Alternative walk climbs back up the path.)* After passing the **central eléctrica**, go a metre/3ft or so up to the left, onto an *acequia.* Walk along it for about 100m, then pick up a path heading upstream. From here you may have to take off boots and socks up to eight times, in order to cross the river! Although it is not very wide, it can be very fast-flowing and icy cold. We have allowed extra time for crossings, but in the dry season there may be no problem at all.

The Dilar Valley — from the viewpoint near the end of the walk (left) and from the promontory reached at 1h52min (right)

Essentially, the path just continues upstream, with crossings coming in pairs to cut off bends in the river. There are numbered WAYMARKING POSTS, usually at crossing points.

The first two wadings may come where the path itself has been washed away (**2h21min**). The valley closes in somewhat and you find yourself walking through trees, with tall cliffs to either side and incredible rock formations ahead. Emerging from the trees, the path becomes stony, running a few metres above river level (**2h44min**) and climbing to an ELECTRICITY POST (WAYMARKING) (**2h50min**). A level stretch takes you across the slopes and through an open area where saffron crocuses blow gently in the breeze. The path then heads past another WAYMARKER and straight up a short gully in the rock face. Steps have been hewn out to make it easy, and you soon reach another electricity post at the top. Whatever the season this is a picturesque spot, always colourful with flowers or berries.

Descend to the waterside again (**3h**) where a further WAYMARKING POST directs you right, to negotiate another two river crossings (**3h04min**). On dry land again, as you cross a shallow, gravelly *barranco* (**3h20min**), look up to the left and see the top of a tower. This is adjacent to the Cortijo Sevilla which you will pass later on. At the head of a second *barranco* a few distinctive pinnacles top a line of cliffs. There are then four more river crossings in quick succession, a 'CAZA' (HUNTING) SIGN after the first (**3h30min**).

With pines standing erect on top of the ridge up to the left, the valley opens up to the right (**4h05min**), and the path passes beneath cables close to WAYMARKING POST 5. Where two valleys meet (**4h14min**), with a wide gravelly *barranco* ahead and to the right, you can either cross the river twice more (but it's much deeper and faster up here), or go up left and clamber, keeping high, round a huge boulder. We prefer the latter option. Back at river level, pick up the path again and pass WAYMARKING POST 6 (**4h35min**) as you go up a slope, now bearing left, away from the river.

Meet a wide earthen PATH (**4h49min**) which runs almost level along the hillside and turn left. (Walk 8 started out on this path on route for Toma del Canal.) Pause at a rocky *mirador* for a different view of the Boca de la Pesca and, after rounding the cliffs of the **Barranco del Buho** (**5h 04min**), climb gradually, to pass to the right of the **Cortijo Sevilla** (**5h25min**). Continue up to a raised area used as a car park. Drop down to the Huenes Valley road (**5h30min**) and turn left. Cut off on a track to the right (**5h38min**); it takes you back to the **Fuente del Hervidero** (**5h50min**).

10 CUEVA DE NERJA • LA CIVILA • CORTIJO ALMACHARES • CUEVA DE NERJA

Photograph page 2

Distance: 17km/10.5mi; 5h08min (almost 1h less if you omit La Civila)

Grade: strenuous, with an ascent (sometimes steep) and corresponding descent of 730m/2400ft. Some rough walking in dry river beds which could be subject to flash floods after rain.

Equipment: see page 51; *boots with ankle support are essential and long trousers are advisable for last section of main walk.*

How to get there and return: 🚗 car or taxi to/from the Cueva de Nerja (starting point of Car tour 3).

Short walk: Barranco de la Coladilla (7km/4.3mi; 1h52min). Moderate, with ascent and corresponding descent of 170m/560ft. Equipment as page 51; access as main walk. Follow the main walk to the 1h05min-point. Turn right on the track and follow it back to the Cueva car park.

Alternative walk: El Pinarillo — Fuente del Esparto — Collado de los Apretaderos (13km/8mi; 3h45min). Moderate, with ascents and corresponding descents of 430m/1410ft overall. Equipment and access as main walk. Follow the main walk to the 1h05min-point, then turn left on the track. When Navachica is visible behind a cleft in the mountains (1h 19min), some reforestation is underway — see how the young trees are protected from the nibbling of the *cabra montés*. Shortly after a series of DAM WALLS to the left, cross a small *barranco* and soon reach **El Pinarillo** (1h29min), a *zona recreativa* with a tiny botanic garden dominated by a statue of a *cabra montés* (photograph page 2). You will return here later but, for now, carry on, noticing the rugged crags at the end of the Cielo ridge on the right before going past a barrier. Cross the **Barranco de la Coladilla** (1h44min), beyond which the track bears left and runs back along the opposite side of the *barranco* from El Pinarillo. Ignore a track coming off the mountain from the right (1h49min). Bearing left, you pass old *cortijo* ruins. Pause to look back, to a tremendous view of the mountains unfolding into the distance. Contour above the *barranco* and reach the **Fuente del Esparto** (1h51min), shaded by eucalyptus and palms, where you can fill your bottles from the spring on the right. As El Pinarillo comes into view again (1h55min) you'll see the helipad and reservoir used for fire control and, closer to the picnic area, an old *era*. Ignore a track to the left (2h) which zigzags back to El Pinarillo and start climbing again on a track lined in spring with rock roses and the little yellow tufts of *santolina* (lavender cotton). After a steep concrete section of path, you reach the **Collado de los Apretaderos** (550m; 2h06min), with fantastic views across the Chillar Valley to the mountains beyond. Go back about 20m and turn right, down a PATH WAYMARKED IN RED. This old mule trail is initially a bit tricky but, as it heads right, it levels out and cuts gradually downhill through low scrub. With binoculars you can make out the glinting cross on Cielo's summit, ahead of you. Cross a TRACK (2h19min) and follow the path as it bears left downhill between large rocks. Crossing the *barranco*, you come into **El Pinarillo**'s sports area. Take the steep path up to the right, to the picnic benches (2h29min). Walk over to the track and turn right: it will take you all the way back to the Cueva car park.

Being so easily accessible from the coast, the Camino de las Minas is busy on Sundays and *fiestas:* El Pinarillo, La Civila and Fuente del Esparto are popular picnic spots. So tackle these walks on a weekday, when you can enjoy the glorious countryside in peace.

Start out from the CAR PARK: walk back down the road as far as the **Hotel Al-Andalus**. Just beyond the hotel, take the PATH which goes down to the right past a concrete structure, crosses a pipe, and bears right across open scrub alive with small birds. You'll see the tall chimney of an old sugar mill as the path winds down to cross the **Barranco de Maro** (**9min**). On the far side, climb a steep stony path. To your left is a close-up view of the **Puente de Aguila**, a 19th-century replica of the great aqueduct at Segovia. This one used to carry water to the sugar mill. At the top of the bank, go right, passing a makeshift HELIPAD on the left and an old white ELECTRICITY HUT on the right. Bear right into pines (**15min**) and start climbing gradually.

Ahead the mountains beckon, Navachica prominent in the background, and the trappings of the coast are replaced by wildflowers, the fragrance of pines and the sound of birds. Hoopoes frequent this particular area, their crests and black and orange plumage rendering them unmistakable. The path levels out (**29min**), before descending into the *barranco* again at the point where it becomes the **Barranco de la Coladilla** (**33min**). Walk along the shady *barranco*, lined with more pines and eucalyptus. Underfoot, deep runnels have been forged by storm water and at either side there are cliffs, pitted with caves and home to families of crag martins. In spring, broom provides occasional eye-catching splashes of colour; this scenic stretch is ideal for a pause. A short steep climb follows (**54min**).

A few minutes later, with the track upstream blocked by a dam, a right fork takes you steeply out of the *barranco*. From the first bend the dam is visible below, and from the second there is a view all the way back down the *barranco* (**1h01min**). Soon (**1h05min**) meet the main track coming up from the Cueva; this is the **Camino de las Minas** which served the many iron mines higher up on the mountains. The main walk (and the Short walk) turn right here. *(The Alternative walk goes left.)* Shortly afterwards, at a NOTICE BOARD, turn left on another track, the **Camino de la Cuesta del Cielo**. *(But for the Short walk, continue straight ahead.)* The *camino* winds up to a crest. After about five minutes, there are three obvious short-cuts which avoid the bends and make for a steeper, but far more pleasant, climb. The first goes left off a right-hand bend and the second and third go right almost immediately after meeting the track again. Thereafter just keep to the track, enjoying views which become ever more spectacular as you make your way to the CREST (**1h46min**). As you begin to descend, a little cluster of cottages is just about visible through a gap ahead. Cross the bed of the **Río Sanguino** and, a little further on, reach a HUT on the right (**1h52min**). You will turn off here later but, if you wish to save almost an hour, skip to the 2h49min-point of the walk. Otherwise continue uphill, eventually reaching the cottages — the **Cortijos de la Civila** (**2h24min**), said to be named after a woman occupant who used to dress as a Civil Guard. Just beyond the last cottage are the ruins of an old bread oven and an *era*. Amongst the prickly pears and the wildflowers, the land is still worked, and the almond trees produce a good harvest. It is a delightful spot and worth the climb.

Retrace your steps to the HUT (**2h49min**); it has been built straight across the path you must now take. So make your way round behind the hut, to where the path is still clear. It descends a bit, then climbs diagonally across the hillside to the brow, from where there are views to Maro and the sea. Your next objective, the Cortijo Almachares, can be seen on the hill ahead. Descend again, through rosemary and a pine wood. Pass the walls of an old WATER TANK and climb alongside an open area with remnants of hunters' fires, to the **Cortijo Almachares** (**3h10min**). This spot is a must for a break. From the other side of the *cortijo* there are far-reaching views down the Sanguino Valley to Maro and Nerja, while the mountains of the Sierra de Almijara and Sierra de Tejeda lie to the west. Perched on rocks up here in the sunshine, we felt close to the gods as we watched first a booted eagle then four short-toed eagles rise from the valley and soar above us. What a sight!

From the *cortijo*, face the sea and turn left. Make for the tall thick PINE TREE that stands alone. Your continuing path runs alongside it and winds down gradually, in places obscured by the bushes overgrowing the sides, but always clear. Beyond a sharp bend to the right, you reach a fork (**3h29min**): take the lower, right-hand path. It descends a bit more steeply, and the vegetation on either side encroaches significantly. The path runs high above the Sanguino Valley on the right, occasionally zigzagging to lose altitude more quickly. It becomes a little indistinct as it takes you into a rocky *barranco* (**3h49min**). But after a few metres (and *before* going into prickly gorse), take a path up to the right which joins the bed of the **Arroyo del Romero** where it runs behind a ruined *cortijo*.

You now have a long walk ahead negotiating the stones, rocks and large boulders in the shady bed of the Sanguino River. Take advantage of the paths which sometimes take you out of the bed and along the banks. The valley opens out for a short while, with an olive grove on the right, then a CAVE on the left (**4h36min**). Giant reeds and lavender grow profusely along this part of the route, and the path takes you along the edge of an olive grove. A cave directly ahead has obviously been inhabitated in the past. Cross the bed again and pass fenced-in ORCHARDS on the left. Return to the river bed and join a track going straight ahead past *cortijos* and orchards. It takes you to the N340 (**4h 53min**). Turn right and, a little further on, go through the green gate in the fencing (if it's open); this will lead you to the cave car park. Otherwise, carry on to the junction and turn right to reach the CAR PARK (**5h08min**).

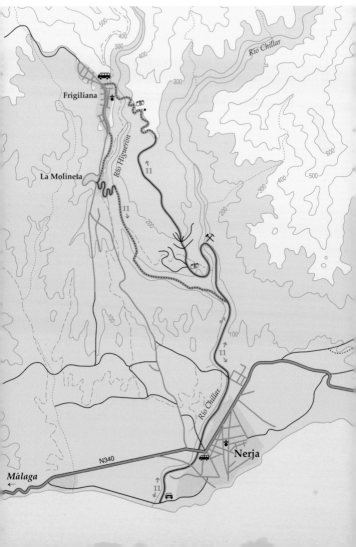

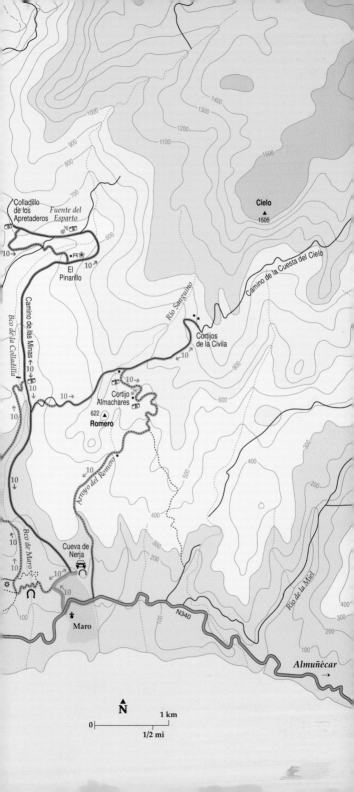

Colladillo
de los
Apretaderos

*Fuente del
Esparto*

10 ←

El Pinarillo

10 →

Bco de la Colladilla

Camino de las Minas ↑

10 ↓

10 ↓

10 →

10 →

↑
10
↓

622 ▲
Romero

Cortijo
Almachares

10 →

Camino de la Cuesta del Cielo

Río Sanguino

Cielo
▲
1505

Cortijos
de la Civila

← 10

1400

1300

1200

1100

1000

900

800

700

600

500

400

300

200

Arroyo del Romero

← 10

500

400

300

200

Bco de Maro

10 ↓

10 ↓

10 ↓

Cueva de
Nerja

10 →

← 10

10

100

✝
Maro

N340

100

Río de la Miel

200

300

400

100

200

300

Almuñécar
→

▲
N

1 km

0

1/2 mi

11 FRIGILIANA

See map pages 88-89; see also photograph page 28

Distance: 16km/9.9mi; 4h41min

Grade: moderate-strenuous; quite long, with ascents and corresponding descents of 500m/1640ft overall, some sections steep. You will usually get no more than the soles of your shoes wet but, after storms or prolonged rains, particularly in spring, you will have to wade, ankle deep, across two or three fords and all the way back down the river.

Equipment: See page 51; *towel and extra socks recommended.*

How to get there and return: 🚌 to/from Nerja (near Car tour 3), then on foot to the mouth of the Río Chillar — on the beach at the western end of Nerja, close to the Perla Marina hotel.

Shorter walks:

1 **Río Chillar** (6km/3.7mi; 1h50min). Easy, with a gentle ascent and corresponding descent of 110m/360ft. Access and equipment as above, but trainers will suffice. Follow the main walk to the quarry (56min) and return the same way.

2 **From Frigiliana to Nerja** (7km/4.3mi; 2h05min). Easy (unless you have to wade down the river) descent of 435m/1425ft. Equipment as main walk. 🚌 from Nerja to Frigiliana (Timetable 5). Pick up the main walk at the 2h36min-point and walk back down to Nerja.

3 **From Nerja to Frigiliana** (9km/5.6mi; 2h36min). Grade and equipment as main walk. Follow the main walk to Frigiliana and return by 🚌 (Timetable 5) to Nerja.

F ew of Nerja's visitors fail to find their way to Frigiliana. Situated high on the hill slopes, this little whitewashed village, shown on page 28, offers hospitality, picturesque scenery, and a glimpse into Andalucía's past. But on this walk, the outward route over the hills gives you an all-encompassing view of Frigiliana that most tourists miss. The return, straight downriver, is more popular but less spectacular. However, it is a favoured bird habitat, and you will be serenaded all the way down by ubiquitous serins. We prefer to tackle this walk in summer or autumn when there is less likelihood of getting our feet wet!

Start by going upriver on the Nerja side of the **Río Chillar**, on a track heading towards the Sierra de Almijara and the conical peak of Cielo (1508m). Pass market gardens and fruit orchards and go under a three-arch BRIDGE (**13min**). After walking under a newer bridge, which carries the N340, you *should* find the going easy. (We found the original little path obliterated by mounds of rubble which, we are assured, will form the foundations of a new track.) Beyond a huge PIPELINE (**26min**) the mountains draw closer, giant reeds line the river on both sides, and late almond blossom blooms well into March. Leave the market gardens behind as the river banks close in (**44min**) and the rocky sides are dotted with caves. A tattered flag flies from a little house built into the cliff, and the WATERFALL shown

Waterfall on the Río Chillar

at the right drops beneath it. Just past a cylindrical water tower, you come to a river junction. The tributary coming in from the left is the **Río Higuerón** (**48min**), named for a fig tree (*higuera*) which once grew near its source. Continue straight ahead on the wide track alongside the Río Chillar. It takes you past a cement works and into a small QUARRY (**56min**), where there is a ford across the river; if it is submerged you will have to wade.

A track, initially concreted, takes you steeply up the opposite bank to the ridge above. With open hills to the right, pass some attractive and colourful villas and *cortijos*; VILLA NO 36 bears a 'Cuidado con el Gato' (Beware of the Cat!) notice on the gate (**1h09min**). Admire the views over fields and orchards in the valley below before turning right at a JUNCTION (**1h16min**) and forking right about 20m further on — up towards a pylon and a small peak. Pass Villa Capricho and go round Casa Sophia to circle between fruit groves. Cross a track and enter an area of open bushland, resplendent with the flowers and the aroma of rosemary at almost any time of the year. When you reach a JUNCTION where four tracks fan out ahead of you (**1h28min**), take the third from the left and head uphill, eventually skirting a fence above a villa. Down on the left is the Higuerón Valley and your return route. Round about here you will begin to see a few RED DOTS AND ARROWS marking the way, and a bit later there are also WHITE PAINT SPLASHES. Continue upwards on a now slightly-overgrown track and lose sight of all habitation for a while as you proceed into the hills. The next houses you see are two valleys away, on the lower outskirts of Frigiliana, and there is still some climbing to do.

As you tramp through a sandy patch, it appears that you are heading away from your destination, but the track soon becomes a narrow rocky path as it heads through some pines and veers back round the head of the first valley. Once across the dip reach the ruins of an old *cortijo* (**2h05min**). From here you can see Frigiliana proper, perched on the hillside, the twin chimneys of its old molasses factory looking drab against the white of all the other buildings. Dating from the 16th century, this building used to be the home of the Counts of Frigiliana. With the village directly ahead, start descending on a narrow path, well marked with RED DOTS. Lavender and rosemary brush against your legs before the path becomes steep and prickly gorse sometimes catches you unawares. But it is not a difficult descent, and you soon reach the clear fast-flowing waters of the **Río Higuerón** (**2h16min**), where a short break beside an oleander tree will refresh and fortify you for the climb into Frigiliana.

Slightly to the right of where you reached the water, look across for the RED DOT which marks the start of the path up the opposite side. Cross the river on the stepping stones (another potential wading point) and follow the path upriver to the right as far as an old shelter, opposite a huge boulder. Go up steps into the SHELTER, pass back under its corrugated iron canopy, and zigzag up a steep path, to cross an *acequia* and reach an even steeper CONCRETE ROAD. Turn right and climb up to **Frigiliana** (**2h36min**), where there are bars and restaurants to welcome you.

You *can* catch the bus back to Nerja (the stop is straight ahead as you come into the village), but the walk turns left, up Frigiliana's narrow main street. Go all the way through the village. Just after leaving (at the point where the lower road comes in from the right), follow the path running along the left-hand side of the road, just beyond a large ADVERTISING BOARD (**2h54min**). The path eventually moves away from the road and descends to cross an *acequia* (**3h**), steepening as it passes the little houses of **La Molineta**. At the junction, just before El Molino de Aceite, turn left down another steep concrete track and wind back down to the **Río Higuerón** (**3h08min**). Turn right downstream. The route is along the pebbly river bed — easy if it is dry, but be prepared to get your feet very wet if there has been significant rainfall. When you reach the junction with the Río Chillar (**3h51min**), cross to the track of your outward route (on rocks and stones). Then retrace your steps to the beach at the western end of Nerja (**4h41min**).

12 FABRICA DE LA LUZ

See photograph page 1 (Cortijo de Buena Vista)

Distance: 9km/5.6mi; 2h41min. (You can shorten the main walk and both short walks by 35min if you drive to the junction at the 18min point.)

Grade: easy, with an ascent and corresponding descent of 260m/195ft

Equipment: see page 51.

How to get there and return: 🚌 to/from the church of Santa Ana in Canillas de Albaida (the 42km-point in Car tour 3); park by the benches.

Short walks: both are easy (essentially flat); access, equipment as above

1   **Fábrica de la Luz** (6km/3.7mi; 1h30min). Follow the main walk to the *fábrica* and return the same way.

2   **Arroyo de la Cueva de Melero** (8km/5mi; 1h50min). Follow the main walk to the *fábrica,* then cross the log bridge below the toilet block. Turn right, upriver (now the Arroyo de la Cueva de Melero) on a charming little path lined with wildflowers. Pass an occasional tiny cultivated plot as you head straight for the hills. Continue until you can't go much further without getting your feet wet and negotiating undergrowth and steep rocks (55min). The path does continue to *cortijos* at the head of the valley, but we turn back here and retrace the route to Santa Ana.

This walk combines the charm of a rural river valley with the delights of a herb-clad hillside. The *fábrica,* an old hydroelectric plant and now an attractive *zona recreativa,* is a particularly popular spot on Sundays and *fiestas.* On a weekday, when it is likely to be deserted, its peace and tranquility are almost tangible.

Start with your back to the main entrance of **Santa Ana**: take the left-hand (lower) of the two tracks straight ahead. It runs fairly level above terracing and an *acequia* 20m below. Olive groves drop down steeply into the valley of the **Río Llanada de la Turvilla** which you will follow for some time. Soon (**8min**) superb views of the Sierra de Almijara and Tejeda open up ahead. The distinctive conical peak is Cerro Atalaya (1256m) and below, to its left, you can just make out the Cortijo de Buena Vista, which you'll pass much later. Reach a JUNCTION where your return route comes in from the right (**18min**; you could park here). Fork left (signposted to La Fábrica), cross the *acequia,* and pass a *fuente* a few moments later. Descending gradually, hear the sound of the river below and catch a first glimpse of the water (**20min**). On a wide bend to the left, you cross a *barranco* with a small RESERVOIR (**25min**) which provides irrigation water for a little *cortijo* on the far side of the river.

Cross a dry *barranco* (**28min**) and start climbing gently. You pass a track (**34min**) which crosses the river at a BRIDGE and heads back high above the opposite bank, then a new track which comes down from a sand quarry. Oleanders line the river banks for a while, and soon the old roofless *fábrica de la luz* comes into view, nestling at the edge of the river, with mountains rising close behind it. Pass it (**46min**) and continue into the well-equipped picnic/camping area (**P**12), where running water and breathtaking scenery make for a delightful break. *(Short walk 1 turns back here, and Short walk 2 crosses the stream.)*

From the FOUNTAIN in front of the recreation building, go up the stone slope and steps, crossing a track and joining a narrow path which winds up above the picnic site. Though steep, it's an easy climb, and rosemary, sage and other fragrant herbs will brush against your legs. Just after a steep rocky step, fork left and climb above an empty water RESERVOIR (**1h**). At one point, through a gap in the hills on the right, you can see all the way back to Santa Ana and along the sierra, from the round mass of Maroma (2065m) almost to Puerto (1824m). Reach a terrace wall, cross it and bear left, to meet a TRACK (**1h21min**). From here there are magnificent views — back over the way you have just come and straight ahead across rolling hills to the coast. Pan right, to take in Málaga's high-rise buildings, then the featureless, brooding mass of Maroma. Now, looking back round to the left, locate a helicopter pad and the almost-hidden Cortijo de Buena Vista, your next landmark.

Turn right on the pleasant track, lined with asphodels; it will take you all the way back to the 18min-junction of the outward route. Listen to the birds and look for the caterpillar trains on the ground, signalling their nests in the nearby pines. Just before reaching the entrance to the aptly-named **Cortijo de Buena Vista**, look for the deep cylindrical pit, probably an old lime kiln, on the right. Shortly thereafter, cross a STREAM on a bend (**1h45min**; the photograph on page 1 was taken here), then fork right. Back at the junction (**2h24min**) bear left for Santa Ana (**2h41min**).

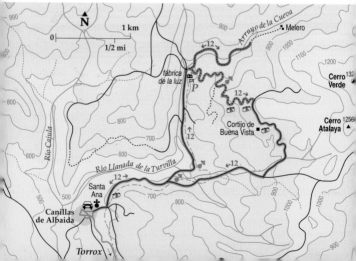

13 ALCAUCIN VALLEY: VENTAS DE ZAFARRAYA TO PUENTE DON MANUEL

Photograph pages 30-31 **Distance:** 15km/9.3mi; 3h51min

Grade: easy-moderate, with a descent of 400m/1310ft.

Equipment: see page 51.

How to get there and return: 🚌 to/from Puente Don Manuel (the 83km-point on Car tour 3); park in the shade under the eucalyptus trees at the junction. Then, from the bus stop close to the *ermita*, pick up the Ventas de Zafarraya 🚐 coming from Torre del Mar (Timetable 6); alight from the bus in the centre of Ventas de Zafarraya, close to the church.

T his walk is not only a birders' delight, but has the added attraction of being almost all downhill! It takes you through countryside where life is lived much as it used to be hundreds of years ago. Don't be surprised to meet old men on donkeys, oxen and horses ploughing in the fields, goats being taken for a walk on leads, or flocks of sheep obstructing the pathways. In spring you'll encounter men high in the branches of olive trees beating the fruit off with sticks, while the women below gather it up into buckets and baskets. You will encounter some noisy dogs en route, but they are either chained, or friendly and timid.

The bus journey up from Puente Don Manuel is an experience in itself. The road winds higher and higher, until you feel as if you are on top of the world. The Boquete de Zafarraya, the huge U-shaped pass between rocky cliffs shown on pages 30-31, looms ever closer as your altitude increases. Just beyond the pass, where the palms and fruit trees of the lower altitudes are left behind, look on the right, and you'll see the path this walk follows close to the road. You may find it a bit chilly in the early morning mists up on this high plateau, but the sun will soon find you as you descend. Take a moment to look at the interesting fountain in the church square before setting off.

Start the walk by leaving **Ventas de Zafarraya** the way the bus brought you in. Pass the PETROL STATION and *pensión* and go under the BRIDGE. This bridge used to carry the rack-railway line to Vélez-Málaga; it was dismantled in the 1960s, but parts of the line still mark the boundary between the provinces of Granada and Málaga. Almost immediately, go off the road to the left, taking the narrow stony PATH which runs alongside the road for a while. A tunnel up on the hillside to the right indicates the continuing route of the old railway line. The path soon veers away from the road and skirts round the foot of tall cliffs, home to choughs and ravens. Nearer ground level, the rocks are alive with small birds including black wheatear and rock bunting. Look down on the Río Alcaucín and the mountain ranges that stretch far into the distance beyond the Embalse de Viñuela. And cast a glance back occasionally at the remarkable sight of the Boquete de Zafarraya.

Just after crossing a dry STREAM BED (**25min**), fork right, leaving the cliffs behind and descending through open countryside. Sage and gorse add a brilliant splash of colour to the landscape in springtime. It's not long before the village of Espino comes into sight, overlooked by the Sierra de Tejeda, a range dominated by the huge barren mass of Maroma. This is a glorious part of the walk. Mountains surround you in every direction, and the air is filled with the sound of stonechats and larks (wood, thekla and sky). Bird song mingles with the sound of goat and sheep bells, as you cross an expanse of grassland (**34min**) and pass a little almond grove, well tended despite its apparent isolation.

When the path becomes a grassy track, notice the old walls of an *era* over on the left. Wind down between cultivated terraces and enter **Espino** at the attractive white-washed *fuente* (**44min**; photograph pages 30-31). Pass the church and immediately fork left on a narrow concreted track which descends past a line of cypress trees to the fields. From a collection of houses called **Las Monjas** (**54min**) continue on what has now become a dirt track. You soon spot the houses of Las Majadas below, and the larger village of Alcaucín in the distance. The track turns sharply left downhill (**1h13min**) towards Las Majadas. Follow it, but notice a track going back off to the right — your ongoing route. In **Las Majadas** (**1h20min**) pass a small orange grove and go down between the houses of this charmingly tiny hamlet. At the bottom, beyond an orchard, make for a tall ELECTRICITY POST and from there take a narrow path down left to the river. (The path is in bad condition and a bit tricky, but just make your way down through the oleanders as best you can.) The sound of the water will lead you to an old sulphur spring and pools, the **Baños de Las Majadas (1h35min)**, used since the times of the Moors.

Retrace your steps back to the houses and then up to the track mentioned earlier (**1h52min**), and head off left at the bend. This old trail, which used to serve the hamlets below, is now used by hunters and shortly becomes a path which rises above an olive grove. On the opposite side of the deep gorge you'll see an *acequia* and a line of beehives close to the Casa del Chocolate.

The rocky path contours high above the cultivated valley, heading directly towards the shimmering waters of

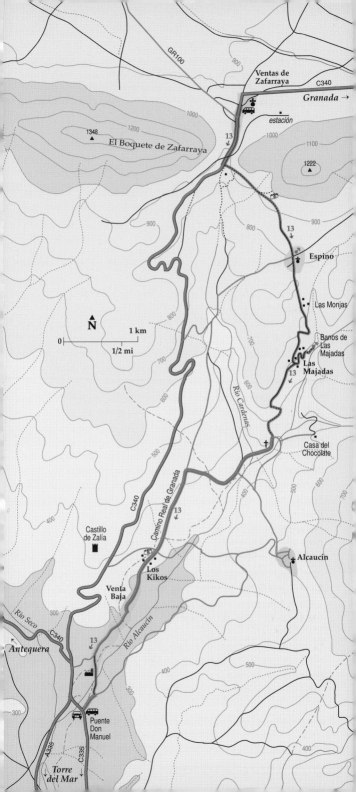

the Embalse de Viñuela in the far distance. Lined with rosemary and violets, the path then descends gently along the top of another olive grove. At the end of this grove, the path becomes indistinct. Follow it as it drops about 5m/15ft down the edge of the grove — onto a clear stony track which continues on towards the *embalse*.* The track brings you out onto a narrow asphalt road with a substantial and decorative SHRINE just to the right (**2h30min**).

Pass the shrine and settle down to enjoy the remainder of the walk which will take you along quiet country lanes, past several houses and *cortijos,* and through olive groves and rural villages. Preoccupied with the sights and sounds of the countryside, you'll soon forget the asphalt beneath your feet. Cross a stream, the **Río Cárdenas**, a lovely spot when the water flows strongly, and begin to climb a little, just for a change. As a road comes in from the right, your road levels out again, and fig trees begin to appear among the olive trees. You are now walking on the medieval **Camino Real de Granada** which runs all the way to Puente Don Manuel. Cross a dip and go straight ahead at a CROSS-ROADS — where another backward look at the Boquete is called for. Descending again, olives give way to citrus fruits, pomegranates and apricots.

Pass between the few houses of **Los Kikos** (**3h20min**) and look over to the right for the ruins of the Castillo de Zalía perched on a hill. Founded by the Phoenicians and reconstructed by the Arabs, little remains of it today. At the far end of the longer village of **Venta Baja** (**3h39min**), fork left downhill, past a workshop and round below an olive oil FACTORY with a tall chimney. A little notice at the fork announces that you are on the ancient route of Ibn Batûta, the 14th-century voyager from Tangiers, who journeyed through southern Spain from Málaga to Granada.

A dirt track takes you between giant eucalyptus trees, across the river and past the factory's residue pools. A little further on it brings you to a road: turn right and follow it to your car at the **Puente Don Manuel** junction (**3h51min**), where you can refresh yourself at one of the many bar/restaurants.

---

*After 30m/yds or so the gradient of this track suddenly steepens to such an extent that you almost feel you are about to fall over a cliff. Like us, you will probably not relish the thought of continuing. So go off the track to the right, passing a LONE TREE and reaching an open grassy slope. The slope is still quite steep, and there is no definite path, but you can easily descend in long gentle zigzags and pick up the track again lower down.

14 PARQUE NATURAL MONTES DE MALAGA: TWO CIRCUITS FROM TORRIJOS

Distance, Grade: see Walk a and Walk b below.

Equipment: see page 51.

How to get there and return: 🚌 to the Torrijos area (the 134km-point on Car tour 4). Or take the C345 out of Málaga or off the ring road at the Olletas exit, signposted to Colmenar. Turn left off the C345 at about the KM544.3 road marker and drive down to the car park near the old white-washed building which is now a museum.

Walk a (Torrijos • Galindo • El Serranillo • Chinchilla • Santillana • Torrijos): 14km/8.7mi; 3h26min. Easy, with an ascent and corresponding descent of 220m/720ft, on good forestry tracks. *Notes begin below.*

Walk b (Torrijos • Pacheco Bajo • Mirador de Martinez Falero • Cuesta de la Reina • Torrijos): 10km/6.2mi; 3h05min. Moderate, with an ascent and corresponding descent of 280m/920ft, some of it prolonged. But good forestry tracks make the going easy. Yellow rings on trees provide waymarking on much of the route. *Notes begin on page 102.*

Short walks: both are easy; equipment and access as above

1 **Pacheco Bajo** (1.5km/0.9mi; 34min). Follow **Walk b** (page 102) to the 19min-point, then turn left on the forestry track. This takes you along the opposite side of the stream, passing the museum which houses old farming implements and machinery (31min). The car park is just beyond the museum (34min).

2 **Santillana** (4.8km/3mi; 1h30min). Ascent and corresponding descent of only 30m/100ft. Follow **Walk b** (page 102) to the 46min-point at Santillana. Return the same way.

Alternative walks: both are easy; equipment and access as above

1 **Bridge below Chinchilla** (6km/3.7mi; 1h52min). Ascent and corresponding descent of 50m/165ft. Follow **Walk b** (page 102) to the 48min-point and turn right at the junction, along the *arroyo*. Within a couple of minutes the ruins of Chinchilla appear up on the right. Continue round to a bridge, where paths run up the steep grassy slopes to the ruins. Chinchilla is private property, however, so just admire it from below and return the same way.

2 **Viewpoint over the park** (7km/4.3mi; 2h10min). Ascent and corresponding descent of 130m/425ft. Follow **Walk b** (page 102) to the *mirador* (1h06min) and return the same way.

This natural park is a botanist's delight, with its mature woodland boasting a huge variety of trees, shrubs and plants. It is also home to over 160 species of living creatures. You may not set eyes on the many small mammals and reptiles, but you will notice the birds, mainly tits, warblers and buntings. In the area now occupied by the park there used to be around a hundred settlements, dating mainly from the latter half of the 18th century. The ruins of some of the old *cortijos* and mills are now reduced to heaps of stones, but others are quite substantial. With the breeze and shade afforded by the elevated position and abundance of tree cover, this delightful walk is one which you will enjoy, even in summer.

Start Walk a by going under the wooden canopy of the

Cortijo Santillana

INFORMATION PANEL and turn right at the first of the PICNIC BENCHES (**3min**). Join a minor forestry road going down to the left and cross the **Arroyo de Chaperas**, to the other side of the benches. Cross the *arroyo* again and wind uphill, alternately in and out of the trees. Ignore a track to the left (**10min**) and continue, climbing gently and enjoying the peace and solitude. It is always beautiful here but, in early spring, when the route is lined with broom, french lavender and gum cistus in glorious flower, the senses are in for a particular treat.

Pass **Cortafuegos Las Jaras** (Rockrose Firebreak) going up to the left (**34min**) and, shortly afterwards, notice, on either side, the distinctive tall bare trunks of maritime pines. A few *quejigos* (Portuguese oaks; see Walk 20) and some cork oaks grow around little streams before you reach a more open level stretch. Here, a track goes diagonally back to the right (**54min**), to the road, and then another forks left to Finca Galindo.

Pause on the next bend for extensive views across the sierras and, shortly after passing the KM4 STONE MARKER turn sharp left around a stream. Here the ground is pitted by the frequent passage of goats from the **Cabrerizas de Galindo**, the white goat sheds down on the left (**1h05min**).

The ruins of Chinchilla, with its sole palm, come into view over on a hill to the left (**1h13min**; see Walk b) just before the KM5 MARKER STONE. The gradient steepens a little before the KM6 MARKER (**1h29min**), and a chain barrier takes you to a major FORESTRY ROAD (**1h35min**). Turn left and pick up a different set of distance markers. At a junction with a little house and a large STONE SIGNPOST (900m; **1h38min**) take the left fork, for Serranillo. From here it's all downhill. Pass a chained road left to El Dorador (a private *finca* down

100

Chinchilla from the Arroyo de Chaperas. When the rest of the area was appropriated by the government for the park, Chinchilla was spared because of the importance of its vines and the plantation of roses which were used in the cosmetics and perfume industry. The land remains private to this day, just one tall palm bearing witness to its former splendour.

in the valley), then one up right to the Casabermeja road. At a JUNCTION marked by a substantial tree (**1h50min**), go left and pass a KM4 MARKER.

A stand of cork oaks circles a clearing on the left before the **Finca de Castañeda** is framed through eucalyptus trees on the right (**1h58min**). Continue past some tempting grassy areas by the roadside, and have a leisurely pause instead at **El Serranillo** (**2h11min**), marked by cypresses and a huge spreading eucalyptus. A grassy promontory runs over the roof of this ruined *casa forestal* and, from a lower level, you can enjoy views over a single cedar tree to the terraces of Chinchilla.

Returning to the track, round the head of a *barranco* and follow it downstream, to cross the **Arroyo de Gutiérrez (2h 30min**), which tumbles over a wall into a clear rocky pool. Ignore a chained track off to the right, and soon find yourself in the setting shown above, very close to Chinchilla. You pass under its slopes after crossing the **Arroyo de Chaperas (2h40min**) using the stepping stones if necessary.

Continue upstream above the *arroyo,* to a JUNCTION (**2h49min**), and fork left (along the outward route of Walk b), passing the ruins of **Santillana** and its old mill-stone close to the KM5 MARKER (**2h58min**). Just beyond the KM6 MARKER you have the choice of crossing the stream (**3h11min**; *P*14a) and following the path along the opposite bank, or continuing along the track. Either way you reach the Torrijos area with an opportunity to visit the museum (**3h26min**).

Start walk b by going under the wooden canopy of the INFORMATION PANEL and take the path going to the left. Pass some picnic benches and continue below the museum, following 'Zona Acampada' signs. A wooden BRIDGE takes you to the camping area and, just beyond the toilet block, you follow a lovely little path along the right bank of the stream, the **Arroyo de Chaperas**. Pass below the ruins of **Cortijo Pacheco Bajo** (**13min**; *P*14a) and within a few minutes cross the *arroyo* on stepping stones to reach a FORESTRY TRACK (**19min**). Turn right and follow the stream for a little longer. *(But for Short walk 1, turn left here.)* The remainder of your route is on forestry tracks, so just relax and enjoy this mature woodland. Surrounded by pines and eucalyptus, you will be accompanied by a blend of aromas as well as the songs of birds. The road crosses the **Arroyo de los Melgarejos** at the KM5 MARKER (**35min**; *P*14b), where broom shines brilliant yellow in the sunshine. At the KM4.5 MARKER (**46min**) you come upon the ruins of **Santillana**, with a path going down to the stream (*P*14c). *(Short walk 2 turns back here.)*

Continuing, reach a junction with another MAP PANEL (**48min**). *(Alternative walk 1 goes right here to look more closely at the ruins of the grand old house of Chinchilla.)* Turn sharp left uphill. Take it easy and let the sights, sounds and smells of the countryside stir your senses. Different views unfold around every bend and, looking over to **Chinchilla** (**1h**), you can almost imagine how it once must have been. A *mirador* on a small promontory (**1h06min**) provides extensive views over the park, and a plaque commemorates one of the park engineers. It bears his epitaph which, roughly translated, reads 'Lord, take unto Thy breast he who sang the glory of Thy wisdom with the ballad of the woods'. *(Alternative walk 2 turns back here.)*

Continuing, reach a major JUNCTION of tracks (800m; **1h29min**). To the right is the Aula de la Naturaleza Los Contadores, an information point and *zona recreativa,* but the walk goes straight ahead, past a map detailing a short walk nearby. (The map is unintelligible and incorrect, so ignore it!). Almost immediately you pass the KM2 marker; continue upwards; on a clear day you'll enjoy magnificent views over to the right. At the next JUNCTION carry straight on (**1h36min**) and keep climbing, pausing to take in views of the Sierra de las Nieves (Walks 17-20) as you round a wide bend to the left (**1h46min**). The track, now called **Cuesta de la Reina** (Queen's Hill), steepens. As soon as you've climbed to an altitude of over 900m, you will see

over to Málaga's port and the west.

Just short of a tall RELAY TOWER, leave the forestry track and take the track which forks left (**1h50min**). (The forestry track continues uphill for about 10 minutes more, past the tower and the relay station to the main road at Fuente de la Reina, where there is a bar/restaurant.) With cables laid underground all the way along it, your 'telefónica' track (as it is locally known) is essentially level and is not waymarked. It provides a very pleasant stroll through a variety of woodland, home to many birds. Look out for the cork oak trees which grow close to the track on either side.

Emerging from the trees after about 3km (**2h35min**), you are greeted by yet more amazing views over the park. Turn left at your original entry road, and head down the steep incline. You catch sight of the MUSEUM below (**2h54min**), before reaching it and your car (**3h05min**).

15 WOODLAND SLOPES

Distance: 10km/6.2mi; 3h08min

Grade: easy-moderate, with an ascent and corresponding descent of 200m/650ft (the only sustained climbing being near the start). At times you may have to go over, under or around fallen trees.

Equipment: see page 51; *carry long trousers, if you wish, for a short stretch of prickly undergrowth.*

How to get there and return: 🚌 to/from Mijas (Timetable 7); alight at the terminus in the main square. Or 🚗 to/from Mijas (the 17km-point on Car tour 5); park in the public car park below the Casa Consistorial and go up steps to the main square.

Short walk: Ermita del Calvario and Cantera del Barrio (3km/2mi; 1h03min). Easy, but it is a short stiff climb of about 120m/395ft to the *ermita*. Access and equipment as main walk, but trainers will suffice. Follow the main walk to the 40min-point, then continue on the track as it bends left and cuts across the lower level of the quarry. At 49min, on a hairpin bend, ignore the steep path which descends directly to the road. Instead, follow the track to the road (55min) and turn left. Pass the *mirador* and, just before the Camino del Calvario, turn right and make your way down into the village (1h03min).

Situated close to the coast with an impressive mountain backdrop, Mijas provides the day-trip tourist with a plethora of souvenir shops, restaurants, bars and *burro*-taxis. Nevertheless, as you make your way up to the Ermita del Calvario, you will realise that it has managed to retain

The Villa Juan Antonio, passed at the start of the walk, is decked out with an amazing array of red and white flower pots.

much of the charm and tradition of a typical Andalusian village. The remainder of the walk takes you through mixed woodland on the slopes of the Sierra de Mijas, where the variety of trees and vegetation is guaranteed to excite the botanist and delight any nature lover.

Start out from the grand white **Casa Consistorial** (town hall), just opposite the bus terminus. With your back to its clock, cross the road, turn left and go around the block into a wooded square. Pass souvenir shops and restaurants and leave the square at the corner, through Pasaje Salvador Cantos Jimenez, signposted to the Centro Histórico. Go up steps and turn left at the top, into the **Plaza de la Libertad**. Almost immediately take the slope, the pretty Calle San Sebastian, up to the right, past the front of the church. As it becomes Calle La Cruz, you will see the words '**Camino del Calvario**' etched into the pathway. This is the start of the pilgrimage which takes you past the 14 stations of the cross, each depicting a stage in Christ's journey to Calvary. With the expansion of the village, only the last half dozen still remain. From here just keep zigzagging up steps, past the Villa Juan Antonio, shown opposite. Just below a pylon, turn right and go up steps to the main road, which runs along the top of the village.

Cross the road and take the stony path which starts just to the right beside a section of wall (**6min**). You can just see the *ermita* above and the path zigzags steeply up to it through pine trees and past the six remaining crosses. When you reach the **Ermita del Calvario** (**16min**; *P*15), look down over Mijas, encircled by its impressive sierra, and you will appreciate just how high you have climbed. Pause for a moment and pick out the village bullring and amphitheatre.

Pass in front of the *ermita* and continue on the path which cuts diagonally up the slope. As the woods thicken, the path steepens a little. When it starts zigzagging, look upwards and locate a little whitewashed dome, the **Cruz de la Misión**, on top of a mound (**28min**). Climb up and take a look. It used to contain a shrine but its door is now closed, with a tangle of electric cables protruding.

Carrying on, the path soon leads to the upper level of the disused **Cantera del Barrio** (**31min**), the local marble quarry. Ignore a track which zigzags down to the left, and follow the path across the quarry and down to the next level. Huge chunks of marble still lie about, providing a backrest for an old man who sometimes whiles away his time there, accompanied by a bird in a cage.

Leave the quarry from this level on a track off to the right but, as it turns left downhill on a concreted section (**40min**), leave it, turning sharp right on a narrow path lined with herbs and lavender. *(But for the Short walk, continue on the track back to the main road.)* For the first few metres the path is a bit tricky, taking you steeply up the left-hand edge of the quarry, but as it turns away from the quarry it widens again, passing a CAIRN at a zigzag to the left.

The path continues rising quite steeply, cutting diagonally left through pines, to meet another path (**45min**). To the right is the quarry, but you go left here and descend for a little while. And now the rest is easy. The path undulates along, always hugging the hillside and mostly shored up by rocks which create a narrow terrace.

Soon (**56min**) you cross (without difficulty) a small rocky landslip and go round a *cañada*. As the terracing disappears and the slope levels out on the left, the path becomes less stony and you may begin to hear the dogs barking and howling in the *perrera*, the municipal dog pound, on the main road below. The terracing comes and goes, and a short break in the trees (**1h15min**) reveals the valley of the Río Fuengirola and hills rolling into the formidable Sierra Blanca (not to be confused with the other Sierra Blanca to the west of Marbella).

Back in the pine woods once more, descend to cross another *cañada* (**1h23min**) and be prepared for a complete and unexpected change in vegetation. This north-facing slope supports a forest of eucalyptus trees and the path, now narrower, somewhat overgrown and damp underfoot, is lined with thistles and prickly shrubs. As the terrain opens out a little, look up to the right to where a radar/weather DOME graces the top of Mijas (1150m; **1h28min**). At this point leave the path you are on (it leads back to the main road) and turn to the right on a NARROW PATH. Fork left almost immediately, as the path to the right heads up towards the ridge. Pines gradually begin to infiltrate the eucalyptus, and the path improves again. Over to the left

a huge water tank stands on top of a hill, with the little white dog pound on the road below it. If you wish to cut the walk short, take the left fork at a major JUNCTION (**1h 40min**). The main walk returns to this spot at the 2h24min-point, but for the present we follow the wide path up to the right through what is now exclusively pine woodland.

At the next JUNCTION (**1h45min**) ignore another route up on to the ridge, and take the left fork, around a *barranco*. In the dampness produced by autumn rains, the usual low shrubs like rosemary and Mediterranean palms soon give way to a variety of colourful mushrooms, some poisonous. The small ones tend to grow in clumps, while individuals of at least dinner-plate dimensions erupt through the soil like mini-volcanoes.

Large spiky aloes grow in an open area undergoing reforestation (**1h 59min**). Just beyond here, at the far edge of the wood, a couple of paths cross a shallow gully and climb up the opposite bank. Take either and find yourself on a grassy plateau with a cylindrical WATER TANK to the left and an almond grove and fig trees up ahead (**2h05min).** Cross to the tank and notice the partially-ruined *cortijo* below. This is also an excellent spot from which to admire again the encircling and impressive Sierra de Mijas, with its crowning radar dome.

It is possible to reach the road, quite a way out of Mijas, directly from here. But if, like us, you prefer to do as little road-walking as possible, retrace your steps to the MAJOR FORK (**2h24min**). Turn right and zigzag down through the trees to the dog pound (**2h30min**). Turn left on the road and, walking along the verge, reach the outskirts of Mijas at a fork in the road (**2h49min**). Go right and walk straight through the old part of the village, between brilliantly-white houses. Some of the streets off to the right have picturesque and interesting signs, like Plaza de los Siete Caños (Square of the Seven Spouts) and Callejo de los Gitanos (Gypsy Alley). It's a long village but you eventually come to a fork at the **Cruz Roja** (Red Cross) building. Head right, to return to the **Casa Consistorial** (**3h08min**).

16 THE BEEHIVE WALK

Distance: 10.5km/6.5mi; 2h55min

Grade: easy, with ascents and descents of only 110m/360ft overall. Stepping-stone river crossings after wet weather.

Equipment for both walks: see page 51.

How to get there and return: 🚌 (Timetable 8; infrequent) to/from the Albergue Municipal at Entrerrios — or go by taxi and catch the bus back. Or 🚗 drive to the *albergue:* From the N340 in Fuengirola take the turn-off for Coín (MA426) and soon after passing Mijas Golf, turn left (5.8km; the 35.6km-point of Car tour 5) and left again (6.4km), both signposted to Entrerrios. Go under a bridge across a wide river bed and through extensive orchards. Shortly after passing between high hedges, you reach the *albergue,* previously a school, now a hostel (9.2km). Park just outside.

Short walk: Arroyo de las Colmenas (4km/2.5mi; 1h28min). Easy and essentially flat, with stepping stone river crossings after rain. Equipment and access as main walk. Follow the main walk to the 44min-point, the ruins of the *casita* with the oven, and return the same way.

The focal point of this walk is the valley of the Arroyo de las Colmenas (Stream of the Beehives), a haven of tranquillity and natural beauty. Its proximity to the coast will be forgotten as you delight in the variety of trees and shrubs and the wildflower wonderland which provide such a rich habitat for birdlife.

Start out by going past the *albergue* and forking right on a DIRT TRACK. It takes you past orchards of citrus fruits, avocados, olives and *nísperos* (medlars). Ignore two tracks off to the right on a left-hand bend (**6min**) and go straight ahead at a junction. Wind down steeply to where the **Arroyo del Laurel** comes in from the left to join the **Río Alaminos** (**15min**).

Cross the Laurel on stepping-stones and turn left alongside a FENCE on a narrow grassy path. The path edges the *arroyo* and becomes a stony track (**21min**), crossing it a few minutes later as the banks close in on the right. You

Calera *(lime kiln) and cork tree (1h08min)*

will have to cross several times more as the path makes its way upstream. Even after substantial rain it shouldn't be particularly deep or difficult, and at times there may be hardly any water at all. This is a sheltered and fertile valley, where wildflowers and herbs bloom most of the year, and the surrounding slopes are usually ablaze with brilliant yellow gorse.

At a junction of streams the track veers right, up the **Arroyo de las Colmenas** (**34min**). Around here are the first of the many *alcornoques*, cork oak trees, which feature on the walk. Pass through a gate and, after a few more stream crossings, head up towards the impressive peaks of the Sierra Blanca (not to be confused with the Sierra Blanca near Marbella).

At a point where the track splits, there is a ruined *casita* (**44min**). It is still in sufficiently good condition for you to be able to see how it was in the past, so take a moment or two to explore. Outside, at the back, is the old *horno*, oven, where bread was baked. *(The Short walk turns back here.)*

From the little house continue along the fork to the left, now on a narrow and fairly overgrown track. Cross a stream and climb gently along a ridge with water flowing on either side. Bear right, past a ruined *cortijo* and solitary tall noble eucalyptus tree (**49min**), then rise steeply into a long-untended olive grove. Continuing uphill, head left to the top of a mound. To the right, stretching behind you, is the Sierra de Mijas and in front of you a road cutting across the slopes of the Sierra Blanca. Once over the mound, you'll see over to the left the dome-like white lime kiln shown opposite. It is still in reasonable condition and worth a closer look: walk a little way past it and then cut off left, eventually picking up a wide path which cuts across a spur between cork oaks. A small path takes you steeply down left to the LIME KILN (**1h08min**). Close by, just a few metres below, ruins of a *casita* overlook a field of fig and olive trees.

Return to the main path (**1h16min**) and continue undulating along the ridge, almost parallel to an asphalt road over on the left. Pass the paltry ruins of a *cortijo* and continue to a crest. Horses are usually grazing in the fields ahead, close to lines of beehives, perhaps the ones that gave the *arroyo* its name. The track bends left round the head of a valley, above what is left of the old **Cortijo de Becerril**, and soon reaches a gate which takes you to the asphalt road (**1h31min**).

The *albergue* is about 5km to the left, but the walk goes

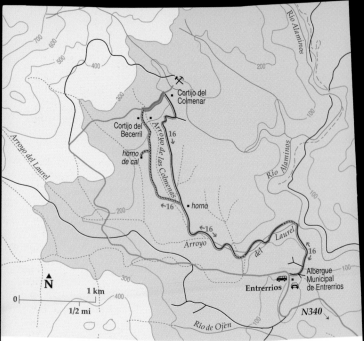

right and passes the horses and beehives before winding across the *arroyo*. Walk back along the opposite bank, high above water level, to a large CAR PARK/LAYBY (**1h43min**). From the far end of the layby take the track which winds up to the right, past a 'Privado' notice, towards a house. (The road continues to the *minas de talco*, talc mines, about half a kilometre further on.) The house, the **Cortijo del Colmenar**, is in use only sporadically but, should any-one be around, ask permission to pass: 'Podemos pasar?'. It will be given, usually with a smile, and you can then follow the track as it rises above the layby and bears left to the top of a slope (**1h48min**).

Descend steeply and meet another track, at a TAPE BARRIER (**1h51min**). Turn right and descend to cross an expanse of low shrubbery and ground cover, delightfully fragrant and colourful. Rise a little, pass through another TAPE BARRIER (**2h05min**) and gradually approach stream level. You come to the HOUSE WITH THE OVEN (**2h13min**) at the junction with your outward route and retrace your steps downstream. Before you know it you are on the narrow path alongside the fence and crossing the stream for the last time (**2h38min**). Head up the steep track to the orchards and from there it's just a pleasant stroll back to the *albergue* (**2h55min**).

17 MARBELLA • PUERTO DE MARBELLA • OLIVAR DE JUANAR • EL CEREZAL • OJEN

Photograph page 42   **Distance:** 12.5km/7.8mi; 4h23min

Grade: moderate-strenuous, with an ascent of 750m/2460ft (some of it steep and prolonged) and descent of 550m/1800ft. Paths and tracks are good, though some may be very wet after rain. The route to the Puerto de Marbella is waymarked in red.

Equipment: see page 51.

How to get there: 🚌 town bus Linea 1 or Linea 3 to the cemetery (Cementerio). Or go on foot: from the Plaza de Toros walk up the Ojén road, past the McDonald's roundabout, over the *autovía* (1.3km) and on to the cemetery, 2.1km). Or 🚗 taxi or car to the cemetery.

To return: 🚌 from Ojén (Timetable 9) to the cemetery or on to Marbella bus station (on the north side of the *autovía*, just west of the Ojén road), or 🚗 Marquez Taxi from Ojén (tel: 288 1280 or mobile: 908 45 52 87)

Short walk: Ojén • Ermita Juanar • El Cerezal • Ojén (5.3km/3.3mi; 1h50min). Easy-moderate, with an ascent (some of it steep) and corresponding descent of 350m/1150. Equipment as page 51, *plus torch for a 100m-long tunnel.* Access: 🚗 or 🚌 (Timetable 9) to/from Ojén; park near/alight opposite the petrol station. From the PETROL STATION walk east along the road for 30m/yds, then cross and climb shallow stone steps beside the **Villa Loli**, onto a rocky trail. Wind high above the groves, keeping the village down on your right. At the end of a short rough section, go straight ahead on a concreted track which comes up from a *cortijo*. It's quite steep, but doesn't last long, soon levelling out and becoming a DIRT TRACK (12min). Up ahead is the Ojén bypass and behind it a pointed rocky peak under which you will pass later in the walk. Cross an *arroyo* and, as the track enters an open area with a *cortijo* on the right, turn up left on a wide stony PATH (16min). Go over some boulders and into a TUNNEL. It's about 100m long and curves slightly to the right. We didn't feel the need for a torch, but it does get quite dark. Emerge from the tunnel and join a small path going straight ahead (SIGNPOSTED 'ERMITA JUANAR'; 21min). It immediately bears right and takes you through a METAL GATE in a goat fence. This marks the start of a fairly steep trail which you will follow for some time. For much of the way, views are limited by the pine trees, so concentrate instead on the ground beneath your feet. Unusually, much of it is sandy, and most of the remainder is carpeted with pine needles. Droppings, footprints and disturbed soil provide ample evidence of the passage of animals, mostly *cabra montés*. Carob pods are plentiful and, when there is any dampness, mushrooms pop up all over the place. As you pass under a huge CLIFF (43min), a sign points right, to the *ermita*, an elaborately-decorated shrine built into the rock face. Back on the main trail, continue uphill and soon start zigzagging, passing the pointed rock you saw from below. Shortly after that, reach a JUNCTION (1h), where the MAIN WALK comes down from the left. Turn right, picking up the main walk at the 3h33min-point and following it back to Ojén.

T his walk winds directly up to the Puerto de Marbella, a 906m/2970ft-high pass through the impressive Sierra Blanca. Close by are the ruins of the Refugio de Juanar, an old hunting lodge formerly frequented by kings and princes. The new *refugio* is now a *hotel parador*. Though steep, the climb is not difficult, and you will be so entranced by the amazing variety of trees, shrubs, herbs and wildflowers that you will scarcely be aware of any fatigue. If you are lucky you may spot an agile *cabra montés* and in this haven for birds, look out particularly for black wheatear on the lower slopes and black redstart higher up.

Start at the *cementerio* (note that this is the cemetery, *not* the cement works which just happens to be alongside it!). Ignore the entrance, signposted to the right; go left, past a few little flower stalls. The road picks up the **Arroyo del Puerto**, a stream you will follow to its source just below the Puerto. At a JUNCTION (**4min**), turn right past Puente Palo 8, the first of a few houses set in mixed woodland.

The road surfacing disappears outside the entrance to the old **Finca Manzah Al Kaid** (**13min**). Continue straight up a track, past a chain, towards crags and peaks ahead.

You pass some flat open areas down by the STREAM (**16min**; *P*17). When you next approach the water's edge (**30min**), the track becomes a rocky and stony trail. Close to the substantial working *cortijo* called **Finca Puerto Rico Alto** a large RED ARROW (**35min**) directs you along the right-hand fork. The trail narrows, with vegetation overgrowing it in places and, as you emerge from some woods, the crags tower directly ahead.

The next section of the trail doubles as a water run-off in rainy weather, so be prepared to paddle along, avoiding as much as you can. It leads up a couple of abandoned terraces to a point where an enclosed concrete *acequia* comes down from above. The path runs up the right-hand edge of the *acequia* but, if it is very wet, take a detour round to the right and join the *acequia* nearer the top, at a WATER CONTROL BLOCK (**44min**). This serves as a signpost, but the writing can be almost obscured by torrents of water.

Before continuing, look back. Marbella seems a long way off and already Finca Puerto Rico is far below you. Lose sight of the valley (**56min**) and wind round on a level stretch above the crags, past citrus groves sitting comfortably in a cultivated mountain plain. Just after passing a ruined *cortijo,* you cross an old *acequia.* If the path is flooded just climb over the roof of the water control block.

Once more in open woodland, go straight ahead for 'Juanar' at a junction (**1h05min**), where Los Monjes is signposted to the left. The gradient steepens as you come out of the woods into an area of low shrubs, bushes and bracken, and you'll see the Cruz de Juanar, a cross, on the rocky peak directly ahead. There is no lack of opportunity to pause and rest as you ascend, but one particularly delightful spot presents itself where the path has come very close to the stream again (**1h21min**). Oleanders overhang a pool of water beneath a huge rock, creating an attractive little corner.

The trail continues to wind up steeply, and Marbella comes into view again for a short time. Go into some pines and notice how sandy the soil is beneath the stones. The terrain becomes more rocky (**1h50min**) as you proceed to a CREST (**2h01min**), from where you can clearly see the pass, your target, ahead. After a short descent, you reach an open sandy area. Ignore the path going off to the left above a wide sloping rock face, and turn up to the right (**2h21min**).

The trail takes you across a region of pale-coloured boulders and up to the **Puerto de Marbella** (**2h34min**) where, suddenly, the world looks different. You find yourself in a level pine wood, with a dirt road running just beyond it. Unexpectedly, picnic benches are set conveniently amongst the trees. After that sustained climb it's at least time for a break, if not a picnic, so make use of them.

The track to the right leads to a *mirador,* but we turn left downhill, towards the triangular summit of Cerro Nicolás. Alongside the Centro de Recuperación e Investigación Cinegética, a hunting centre, magnificent chestnut trees front the ruins of the old hunting lodge, the **Refugio de Juanar (2h50min)**. A little further on, extending along both sides of this forestry track, is the **Olivar de Juanar**, a vast and still very productive olive grove. At the end of the grove (**3h08min**) the track makes a sharp bend to the left. If you were to continue you would come, in about 15 minutes, to the new Refugio de Juanar, set at 780m. You can get a drink or a meal there if you wish, but it's expensive. Leave the road and turn off to the right just before the bend. Ignore two paths going to the left and take the one going straight ahead, at right angles to the road. It's an enchanting path, another old trail, quite steep with sandy soil and a carpet of pine needles making it mostly soft underfoot.

At a JUNCTION (**3h33min**), the Ermita Juanar is signed to the right *(the Short walk comes up here),* but head left for El Cerezal. Wind down into the valley past an 'EL ARENAL' SIGN, ravaged with time, which draws your attention to a particularly sandy slope (**3h40min**; photograph page 42). Begin to follow a *barranco,* criss-crossing it several times before seeing the huge holding wall of the *autovía* directly ahead. Go through a short TUNNEL (**3h53min**), across a grid and through a gate in the goat fence. Now another surprise awaits you: formerly a *cortijo,* **El Cerezal** (**3h55min**) has been transformed into a charming *zona recreativa* set on several levels. Add a shrine to Nuestra Señora del Pilar, a running stream, and a tiny lemon grove, and you have just the place for a short break before returning to 'civilisation'.

A narrow road takes you downstream, past a line of cypress trees, to the MAIN ENTRY GATE. Pass through it and almost immediately wind round to the right at a JUNCTION. A *cortijo* sits to the left of an open area (**4h09min**) at the foot of the slopes, and three routes lead out from the far end. Ignoring the track which goes straight on and the path which goes up the slopes to the right (the outward route of the Short walk), take the middle route, a rough rocky track, cemented in places. As it bends sharply left, go straight ahead on a path which descends to the road at the side of the **Villa Loli**, near the PETROL STATION/BUS STOP (**4h23min**).

18 ISTAN

Distance: 22km/13.6mi; 6h34min

Grade: strenuous and long, with an ascent and corresponding descent of 430m/1410ft. Mostly on good paths and tracks, but with one awkward descent on a steep, rocky, indistinct and overgrown path.

Equipment: see page 51; *a compass could be useful and also a towel if there has been rain.*

How to get there and return: 🚌 (Timetable 10; infrequent) or 🚗 to/from Istán (the 15.5km-point in the Istán detour on Car tour 6); park in the car park at the entrance to the village.

Short walk: Outlook over the Río Verde valley (7km/4.3mi; 2h09min). Easy, with an ascent and corresponding descent of 120m/395ft. Access as main walk; equipment as page 51. Follow the main walk to the 1h-point, then fork down left on a good track affording fantastic views into the Río Verde valley. Pass under cables and reach a JUNCTION (1h10min), where the main walk comes in from the right. Turn left, picking up the main walk at the 5h35min-point and following it back to Istán.

M uch of the melting snow from the high peaks in the Parque Natural Sierra de las Nieves drains into the Río Verde and collects in the Embalse de la Concepción, just west of Marbella. Istán sits above the northern tip of the reservoir, and this circular walk takes you from there into the southern region of the park. The abundance of water creates a series of fertile mountain valleys between slopes which support a huge variety of trees and shrubs. The scenery is always magnificent but, after the winter snows, when the peaks are dazzlingly-white, it is even more splendid.

Begin the walk at the CAR PARK: follow the steep road up to the 'Polideportivo' (sports complex). Just after it becomes unsurfaced, fork left (**6min**) for Monda and Tolox. This narrow dirt road contours under the western slopes of the Sierra Blanca and will take you all the way to a pass, the Puerto

On the track near the sign warning of beehives, with the Sierra de Canucha in the background

de las Carreteras. The gradient is fairly gradual, with just one or two steeper parts, and the easy walking enables you to relax and enjoy the delightful views that greet you around every bend. Across a little valley with green terraces and orange groves well irrigated by an *acequia*, Istán looks particularly attractive (**13min**).

As the dirt road veers right (**38min**), ignore a concreted track going steeply back left to a *cortijo* on the lower slopes. Around November, olive trees growing along the verge are laden with fruit of differing colours. Close to a white house a track comes in from the right off the **Cuesta del Alcornocal** (Cork Oak Hill; **58min**). At a junction (**1h**), follow the dirt road up to the right. *(But for the Short walk, go left.)* The grey peak of Torrecilla (1919m) rises beyond the Sierra de Tolox and, beyond another fertile valley, a sharp rocky peak on the Sierra de Canucha comes into view to the right.

A tiny house is tucked into cultivated slopes below the dirt road, and several others are set up a track to the right — above the banks of the **Arroyo de Castaño** (**1h25min**). The road forks right at a JUNCTION (**1h30min**) and runs parallel to electricity cables high above the valley of the Arroyo de Alcornoque (Oak Stream), with its triangular orchard. Further up this becomes the Arroyo del Portugués, and you will see both again later as you return along the opposite side of the valley.

Pass a track up right to a *cortijo*, go under the cables, and pass two other tracks to the left, the first of them chained off (**1h48min**). Rounding the next *barranco*, you'll see the line of cables running through the pass and several *cortijos* set in another mountain valley. You pass the entrance to one of them, **Casa del Moreno**, just alongside a pylon (**2h01min**). A further mountain valley with terraced slopes opens up around the wide rocky bed of the **Arroyo de la Cañada del Infierno** (**2h10min**). The dirt road crosses the stream bed a couple of times as it winds up alongside

the valley, passing under CABLES again (**2h41min**), before eventually reaching the crest at the **Puerto de las Carreteras** (600m; **2h54min**).

Survey your surroundings, then leave the dirt road by going left on a track. (The road veers right and continues all the way through the park to Monda and Tolox.) The good track runs through cork oak woods, through a wild landscape dominated by the stark mass of Torrecilla. Soon (**3h08min**) fork up to the left on a rough forest track and cross a WIRE BARRIER. The valley of the Arroyo del Portugués soon opens out on the left, your outward route visible along the opposite bank. Ignore a track up left to groves (**3h20min**) and descend through more cork woods. A variety of shrubs and bushes, including heather, grow along the verge, and in late winter you will see the fallen fruits of the *madroño* (wild strawberry tree).

Over on the right, a derelict *cortijo* perched on a mound is dwarfed by the mighty Torrecilla (**3h30min**). As the track bends right and deteriorates, Istán is clearly seen ahead, and a 'PELIGRO COLMENAS' NOTICE warns of beehives ... but we didn't see any. The track becomes a delightful PATH (**3h45min**) which varies in width and surface. Jays cackle overhead and, on this more humid (north) side of the hill, the vegetation is lush and sometimes encroaches on the path. Tall spindly stalks of fragrant gum cistus line the route, leaves and stems sticky to the touch. Among them, the berries of mistletoe, *madroños* and berberis add small splashes of colour to the various shades of green, and mushrooms pop up through the soil.

The path appears to end suddenly at a small CLEARING (**4h08min**), but turn sharply right and you will be able to spot it by the side of a large cork oak. It descends steeply through the undergrowth, over stones and pine needles. This is the start of the nasty bit. As the path remains overgrown and indistinct, just keep going straight ahead in a westerly direction, only deviating to avoid things growing or fallen over the path. Descending a little spur, after a while you will begin to hear the sound of water ahead of you, but still far below. The **Río Verde** comes into sight just as you notice a track down on the left (**4h48min**). When the path ends, clamber down a metre or two to reach it.

Turn left, passing below the route you have just walked, then go past a chain to the edge of the **Arroyo de Alcornoque** (**5h06min**). Here, where the track is sometimes submerged, you cross the stream. At a JUNCTION (**5h13min**) go straight on, bending away from the river. Cross the **Arroyo del Castaño** and pick up the CABLES again (**5h31min**). At a JUNCTION (**5h35min**; *the Short walk comes in from the left here*) go right downhill through pines. Ignore a very rough track going up to groves on the left (**5h43min**) and another down to a *cortijo* on the right (**5h48min**). Leaving the cables behind, the track takes you up through orchards of citrus fruits, avocados and *chirimoyas* (custard apples). Notice some interesting rocky pinnacles on the right.

When you reach a steep section (**6h11min**) take it easy, keeping an eye open for the old mill down in the valley. Ignore a path coming in from the left just before a *casita* and follow a concrete section of track across a bridge over a stream. Entering Istán (**6h26min**), turn up left and round to the CHURCH SQUARE. It's probably too late now to picnic but, just a short distance away, there's a good spot for a break (*P*CT6b). Otherwise, go left alongside the Bar Sud America and up the steep slope to the right of the pretty *lavadero* and *fuente*. This leads directly into the CAR PARK (**6h34min**); the bus stop is in the main street just below.

19 RIO DEL BURGO

Distance: 19km/11.8mi; 4h51min

Grade: strenuous (because of the length), with ascents and corresponding descents of 260m/850ft overall. Good paths and tracks throughout.

Equipment: see page 51.

How to get there and return: 🚌 to/from El Burgo, the 86km-point on Car tour 6 (or drive directly from Marbella via Coín); park near the bridge on the southern outskirts of the village.

Shorter walk: The 'cathedral' (13km/8mi; 3h20min). Easy, with a gentle ascent and corresponding descent of 150m/490ft. Access and equipment as main walk. Follow the main walk to the 1h40min-point (our 'cathedral with organ pipes') and return the same way.

Short walks: both are easy; access and equipment as main walk.

1 **To the first weir and reservoir** (4km/2.5mi; 1h15min). Gentle ascent/descent of only about 50m/165ft. Follow the main walk to the 38min-point and return the same way.

2 **El Burgo • Fuensanta • El Burgo** (6km/3.7mi; 1h46min). Ascent and corresponding descent of 100m/330ft *each way*. Follow the main walk to the 13min-point between the two villas. Turn left on the narrow stony old trail linking El Burgo with Fuensanta. Climb between cultivated fields and olive groves and walk along a couple of level terraces. Once out on the slopes, the path doubles as a water run-off and will be muddy after rain. Reach a CREST (40min) and descend straight ahead. Take any one of several paths through the pines (but make sure you keep to the right of the main water course), until the single path eventually becomes more obvious. Go right at two forks, and pass a deep ravine dropping away on your left (49min). After alternate steep and level stretches you will see Fuensanta below, and any of the paths will take you down to the track, just to the right of the old MILL AND PICNIC AREA (55min). Return the same way; if necessary, follow notes from the 4h-point in the main walk.

Set in the northern region of the Parque Natural Sierra de las Nieves, this river walk is delightful at any time of year. Tits, black redstarts and other small birds are plentiful, and colour is provided by wildflowers in spring and the rich reds and golds of the trees in autumn. Because it's so shady, the walk can even be pleasant in summer. And although Fuensanta may be teeming with visitors at weekends and *fiestas*, at other times it is blissfully tranquil.

Start out from the Yunquera side of the old BRIDGE across the **Río del Burgo**. Take the track down off the road and, with the river on your right, follow it upstream through cultivated fields and olive groves. A very gradual incline takes you past the **Villa El Quinto Pino** and **Villa Ponce Vera** (**13min**). The narrow stony trail between the two villas will be your return route. *(But Short walk 2 turns left on the trail now.)* Carry on past the METAL FENCING (**19min**) which marks the last of the smallholdings. The track, now some metres above river level, heads towards the hills. Pines grow on the slopes while deciduous trees line the river banks.

At the first of several weirs (**31min**), water cascades from

119

a reservoir down into a lagoon, a popular bathing spot in summer. A rocky promontory overlooks the weir, and from this point a chained-off track goes down to the waterside and another lagoon (**38min**; *P*19a), goal of Short walk 1. Continue on the main track, ignoring another which crosses the river to a small *molino* (mill) further along.

The valley narrows for a while, with cliffs on the left. A *cortijo* on the opposite bank is particularly pretty in autumn (**44min**), and curious pyramid-shaped structures stand outside another *cortijo,* in ruins at the side of the track. Climb quite high above the river and, after passing a deep gorge on the far side (**54min**), look out for a very sheer, orange-coloured section of cliff (**58min**). Perched on top, overlooking another weir and reservoir, is the white monument at the Mirador del Guarda Forestal on the road between El Burgo and Ronda.

The river flows through a deep, narrow channel far below as you enjoy a fairly straight and level section of path (**1h20min**), before descending a little, then rising past a *casita* with animal shelters (**1h29min**). Set above yet another weir and protected by noisy but harmless little

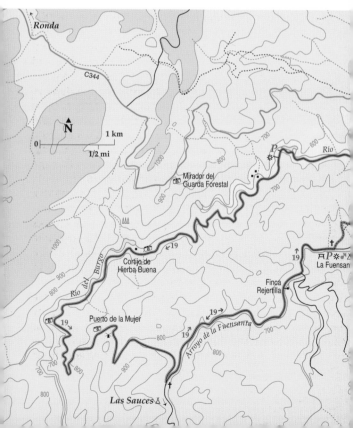

dogs, it is just used for the daily tending of sheep and goats. Soon (**1h35min**) you're in the setting shown overleaf, passing above clear, sparkling lagoons overlooked by a spectacular rugged outcrop which, from a little further on, resembles a 'cathedral' tiered with organ pipes. There's another charming spot down at river level (**1h40min**), pleasant for a pause on the pebbly banks or in the shade of pines. *(The Shorter walk turns back here.)*

Up to this point the track has been gently undulating, but it now begins to climb steadily. Stop for breath as the track turns left and contemplate the valley that opens out on the right (**1h52min**). Encircled by mountains, and wooded with pines, it is traversed by a deep gorge running between steep and pronounced cliffs. The upstream section of the river is left behind when another left-hand bend (**2h11min**) takes you back, high above your original route, through trees which provide cooling shade for a while. Emerging into the open again, pause briefly for a view back through the gorge (**2h23min**) and take a welcome rest when you reach **Puerto de la Mujer** (Woman's Pass; **2h30min**), complete with helipad.

Now the long but pleasant descent begins. Views are dominated by the rugged silhouette of Prieta (1521m), and on the ground you might see giant mushrooms, especially in autumn and winter. A tall STONE CROSS marks a junction with a forestry track (**3h01min**), where Las Sauces, a camping area, is some 3km to the right. Turn left and follow the **Arroyo de la Fuensanta** downstream. There's still a long way to go, but it's almost all downhill through delightful shady woodland. Sunlight filters through the trees and the sound of running water and bird song keeps you company. Pass the track which crosses the river to the large **Finca Rejertilla** (**3h39min**). Some minutes later a notice by a footbridge proclaims the *finca* is an 'English and country seat'.

Just as you enter **La Fuensanta**, there is a track up to the left, marked by another tall STONE CROSS (**4h**). This is your onward route, but first explore this delightful *zona recreativa* built around an old mill (**P**19b). Then turn up the track by the cross but, almost immediately, cut off right on a path (indistinct at first) which runs up alongside a little gully. The path becomes more obvious and wider as it winds up through pines, then levels to contour around the slopes. At a fork (**4h08min**), where there is a deep *barranco* on the right, take either path (the path to the left is a little less steep and again follows the gully). At the top of this climb, meet a path and turn left. Contour round and rise to a crest, from where El Burgo can be seen in the valley below. Go left and descend on a stony old trail, through olive groves and cultivated fields. When you reach your outgoing track on the banks of the **Río del Burgo** (**4h39min**), turn right and follow it back to the BRIDGE and your car (**4h51min**).

Lagoon below the 'cathedral'

20 PEÑON DE LOS ENAMORADOS (LOVERS' ROCK)

See also photograph pages 6-7

Distance: 16.5km/10.2mi; 4h40min. Allow an extra half hour if you wish to climb the Enamorados peak.

Grade: strenuous, with ascents and corresponding descents of 500m/ 1640ft overall. On one section there is no definite path, and care is needed in navigation.

Equipment: see page 51; *walking boots and compass essential.*

How to get there and return: 🚗 to/from the Quejigales entrance to the Parque Natural Sierra de las Nieves beside the km136 road marker (the 47km-point on Car tour 6). Drive along the dirt road, where peonies bloom in May, past the Conejeras area (marked by a board; 2km; *P*20). Ford a usually-dry watercourse and immediately fork left. Fences, grids and gates (usually open) control the passage of the *cabra montés*. Veer left at Cortijo la Nava and follow the road as it winds upwards, becoming partially surfaced (5.5km) with some potholes and unprotected drops. Ignore the right turn to Puerto de las Golondrinas (6km) and reach a fork at a height of 1311m (signposted; 9km), where right leads to the Puerto de los Pilones. Go left to the Quejigales camping/picnic area (10km) and park in the enclosure at the ranger's building or on the grass just beyond it.

Short walk: Ranger's monument (4km/2.5mi; 1h). Easy, with an ascent and corresponding descent of 130m/425ft, all on tracks. Access and equipment as main walk. Follow the main walk to the 31min-point and return the same way.

Alternative walk: Puerto de los Pilones (7.5km/4.7mi; 2h30min). Strenuous, with an ascent and corresponding descent of 450m/1475ft. Access and equipment as main walk, but compass not essential. From the Quejigales building walk back along the road and take the track up to the left (by the sign indicating an altitude of 1311m; 10min). Pass through a chain barrier and start the long but gentle, winding climb, pausing for breath at a viewpoint (20min). Gorse, then pines, accompany you as far as a sharp bend to the left (1411m; 28min). Continue in full sunlight until you pass under a few shady *pinsapos* (48min). You will marvel at the sierras lined up one behind the other in almost every direction. Then the whole Quejigales area and Cortijo la Nava come into view (1h05min). The walk continues down a steep path to the left (1h21min), but it's worth continuing for about 50m/yds to the **Puerto de los Pilones**. Then pick up the main walk at the 3h33min-point and descend somewhat more steeply to your car.

I t is essential to choose a clear, calm day to get the best out of this exhilarating and highly-satisfying mountain walk in the heart of the park. Make sure you are properly equipped for the conditions. From January to March, snow can drift up to a metre deep on the slopes of Enamorados and, at other times, the altitude can mean scorching sun or very chilly temperatures. But it's always beautiful. The sight of the cushions of hedgehog broom, spines encased in ice, sparkling like jewels in the brilliant sunshine of mid-November, is never to be forgotten. The start of spring heralds a different spectacle, with the *pinsapos* sprouting bright green buds from the ends of every branch, and wildflowers begin to carpet the hillsides. As for wildlife, apart from the beautiful horses that roam free in the park, you are quite likely to spot small herds of ibex and, if you are lucky, a *meloncillo* or North African mongoose.

Start out by going along the road past the PICNIC BENCHES AND CAMPING AREA. Pass through a chain barrier, to an INFORMATION PANEL which marks your return path across the stream from Puerto de los Pilones. Ignore a track off left (**6min**) and continue upstream, on a gradual incline, through fragrant pine woods. Shortly after the track veers right into open grassy countryside (**15min**), pines begin to be replaced by the distinctive shapes and darker foliage of *pinsapos*. Another INFORMATION PANEL (**16min**) marks the start of a track to the right: take this, and circle under towering cliffs, to a concrete WATER CONTROL POINT (**26min**). Up to the right, a STONE MONUMENT commemorates a ranger who devoted his life to protecting the *pinsapos* and a little further on retaining walls try to prevent erosion. The track deteriorates into a rough path, crossing a little gully before starting to climb steadily (**31min**). *(The Short walk turns back here.)*

Continue circling uphill below the crags, re-membering to take it easy at this altitude. The local people say you should '*subir como un viejo, para llegar como un joven*' — 'climb like an old man, to arrive like a youngster'. Entering *pinsapo* woodland (**44min**) look out for short-toed tree creepers and the ibex that often gather here. Through the trees, notice the barren rocky mass of the Sierra de la Hidalga (1407m) over to the left (northwest) — and a vast limestone wall of rock ahead (**46min**). Contemplating the magnificent and ancient *pinsapos* that form this area of woodland, it is easy to understand why they are accorded special status.

Descend gradually through the wood, to a point where Cerro Alto looms ahead through a gap (**50min**). To its left, and perhaps best described as a hemispherical rocky dome, is your goal, the isolated peak of Enamorados. Beyond a couple of CLEARINGS (**54min**) the path steepens, winding down to run along the base of a rocky slope on the right, through some prickly shrubbery and across rocks. A CAVE is set into the rock face (**1h06min**) not long before the massive bulk of the limestone wall comes into sight once again, now just ahead.

The path, a little indistinct, rises up the side of the wall over rocks and stones and, passing to the left of a CAIRN, it soon comes alongside a stream bed. Water sometimes flows strongly here, giving birth to delightful little water-falls, but often there may be scarcely a trickle. Follow the stream up across some rocks. When you see a STONE TROUGH on the opposite bank, to the left, cross over to it (**1h20min**). Pause to refill water bottles from the *fuente* which keeps it topped up and rest before the next stage of the climb.

From the top end of the trough climb up diagonally to the right. There is a path of sorts, but you are likely to keep losing it. Although the slope is steep it's quite easy going as you just head upwards across the rocks, picking your way between low gorse bushes. You will soon see a dead TREE STUMP above you, with a tall HEAP OF ROCKS to its left. Pass to the right of both, heading roughly northeast, towards the left-hand end of the saddle you see ahead. Zigzagging eases the gradient and, passing to the left of a rocky shoulder, you should eventually locate the reasonable path which takes you on to the grassy SADDLE at almost 1600m (**1h49min**).

Before picking up the narrow path that runs along it to the right, take a moment in this lovely spot to absorb the extensive views which greet you. Just below, steep cliffs drop into the valley; ahead are the lakes of Los Chorros, near Antequera; round to the left is the Sierra de Grazalema (Walks 21-23); and, to the right, Enamorados rises alongside Cerro Alto.

Here you see the first of the hedgehog broom, a low spiny cushion-like shrub which carpets much of the next part of the route. Characteristic of the highest mountains of southern Europe and North Africa, it usually grows between 1700m and 2000m, sometimes called the 'hedgehog zone'. Interspersed with the broom are the distinctive dark spiky leaves and bulbous light green flowers of the unfortunately-named, but eyecatching, stinking hellebore.

Set off, following the path as it heads round the far side of the closest hill (roughly southeast) and climbs diagonally up its bare rocky slope, home to noisy choughs. The path crosses a small gully (**2h01min**) and heads upwards to a CREST (**2h08min**). Follow it straight ahead towards the next ridge, with Enamorados rising majestically over to the right. As you skirt a rock wall on the left and cross an open expanse of grassy slope (**2h16min**), you come upon a wonderful sight. You will suddenly find the whole of this book laid out before you. From left to right almost every sierra is visible, from Grazalema all the way round to the magnificent Sierra Nevada. For much of the year this latter at least will be snow-capped, adding to the fairytale panorama. We have seldom seen such an awe-inspiring view; *now* you realise why we recommended a clear day.

When you are ready to move on, continue eastwards (straight towards the Sierra Nevada) along the path for 20-30 metres, but turn off at a CAIRN, where a path goes diagonally back to the right (it is indistinct at first, but marked with more CAIRNS). It crosses a stony slope and climbs to another path, running along the Enamorados ridge — the **Camino de las Nieves** (**2h30min**). Cerro Alto rises beyond the dome, and the Torrecilla ridge is across to the left. Its main peak, the highest point in the park (1919m/6295ft), rises at the right-hand end of the ridge. Just below, looking almost dead, semi-evergreen oaks grow in a sloping *nava* (grassy mountain plain). These are the first of the many *quejigos*, Portuguese oaks, from which the area derives its name. The path takes us down to the left of the rocky dome of Ena-

This well-restored nevera (snow pit) is passed at about 3h30min. It was used to collect snow which was compacted and cut into ice blocks — the old form of refrigeration.

morados (1780m). However, if you are keen to conquer the peak (about 20m/65ft of scrambling) or to just sit on the rocks beneath the dome, leave the path and cut off to the right here (**2h34min**). It's as good a picnic spot as you'll find anywhere, with views extending over more meadows of *quejigos* to the Sierra de Mijas and the coast.

Continuing, the path heads round above the *quejigos,* leaving Enamorados behind. Bear left to a grassy patch and, after going over a rise, watch out for the deep unprotected CAVERN to the right of the path (**2h50min**). Cairns line the path as it passes across rocks and descends to a dip, from where several indistinct paths snake up the other side. Just head uphill and across the saddle ahead, to a FLAT AREA where water often collects (**3h04min**). The path is clear again and takes you through large clumps of heather, to a LARGE CAIRN in a small clearing. Head right, passing close to some *quejigos* which, in November, gave us quite a shower, when the ice encrusted on their branches melted in the afternoon sunshine.

Ignore paths to the left which lead to the summit of **Torrecilla** (**3h10min**), a popular, but we think boring, walk, frequented by the locals on Sundays. Continue climbing and pass the huge *nevera* shown above. Notice the water control walls across streams down on the left, and continue across a grassy expanse under a relay tower and up to the track at the **Puerto de los Pilones** (**3h33min**). Views across the sierras are magnificent and, on a clear day, you'll see Gibraltar and the North African coast. Turn left down the track, but leave it within about 50m/yds: take a clear path which descends to the right. It zigzags down open slopes through the **Cañada del Cuerno** (Horn Ravine; photograph pages 6-7), becoming steeper as it passes through a forest of *pinsapos* (the huge roots of these trees provide convenient footholds on the long descent). Once out of the trees (**4h16min**), Quejigales is visible below and the rocky slopes give way to an often-muddy area through pines. Stepping-stones take you across the STREAM and on to the track at the INFORMATION PANEL. Turn left, pass the campsite and reach your car (**4h40min**).

21 GRAZALEMA • MERENDERO DEL BOYAR • LLANO DE LAS PRESILLAS • LLANO DEL ENDRINAL • GRAZALEMA

Distance: 8km/5mi; 2h36min

Grade: moderate, with ascents and corresponding descents of 300m/ 1000ft overall (some steep sections). Some care with navigation required in places.

Equipment: See page 51; *walking boots essential.*

How to get there and return: 🚌 to/from Camping Tajo Rodillo (the 88km-point on Car tour 7); park opposite the campground. Or on foot from Grazalema: walk up to the road that runs above the village; the campsite is just a short distance to the right.

This is an exhilarating walk which contrasts the gentleness of a river valley and a mountain meadow with the Llano de las Presillas, a wild and remote plain covered with strange sharp rocks eroded by the elements. In late spring and summer these same rocks provide anchor and shade for delicate wildflowers.

Start out from the CAMPSITE ENTRANCE and walk up the road for about 300m/yds. At the **Río Guadalete (5min)**, sometimes dry at this point, go down left, cross the river and follow the path alongside it. Keep left at a fork (**8min**), beyond which the path widens for a while, becoming a partially-cobbled trail which runs between the road and the river. With the sound of bird song and trickling water and the attractive oleanders along the bank, the road is scarcely visible and almost forgotten. Where the road makes a hairpin bend close to the trail (**14min**), cross a stream on a path which passes to the right of a CIRCULAR STONE TABLE and stools. After rising between gorse bushes, the path eventually brings you to the ROAD again (**39min**) and continues on the opposite side, heading diagonally up to the left. At a fork, you will notice a building over to the left — the *merendero* (picnic shelter). It is set back from the road about 50m below the Puerto del Boyar where a *mirador* offers extensive views over the *parque natural.*

The right fork leads to the Puerto, but the walk goes left, reaching the road again just opposite the *merendero* (**45min**). Go through the gate to its left, near the source of the Río Guadalete, and follow BLUE ARROWS straight ahead across a gully and onto a straightforward, but fairly steep and rough, rocky path. At the top of the slope (**54min**) it bends right and passes through a gentle area of grass and pines (*P*21). The path then becomes stony for a while, as it runs alongside rocks on the left and climbs steeply. Then gorse lines the route, and the gradient lessens, while views open up over the valley ahead (**1h06min**).

A level grassy stretch, dotted with sharp rocks, leads you to a gradual rise between boulders. When you begin to descend slightly, you may see a cairn on top of a low rock to the left, as the *path virtually disappears* at **Llano de las Presillas (1h15min)**. Make sure of your ongoing route here, before relaxing to enjoy the scenery. With the twin peaks of Simancón and Reloj rising majestically ahead in the Sierra del Endrinal, bear right across the plain until you can see a FENCE ahead — you will not need to walk far. With

Peñon Grande, from the rustic cortijo *near the end of the walk*

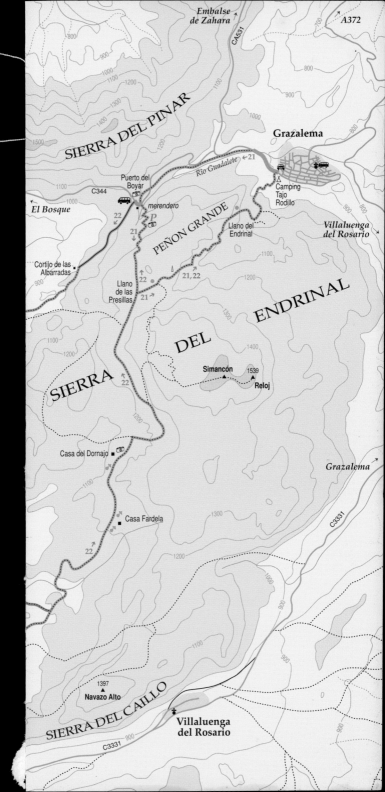

the fence about 100m ahead of you, look left and locate a cairn on top of a high rock, towards the east. Your continuing path starts to the left of that CAIRN (**1h18min**). You should be able to pick the path out amongst the rocks as it heads directly towards a singular pointed peak, then bears slightly left to pass a *nevera* (snow pit; **1h20min**). About 100m along the path, notice a large circle of stones down below on the left, an old *era*. From here the path descends slightly and, if you pay attention, you'll see it split after just a further 80m or so. The right fork leads to the summits, so take the left fork (**1h24min**), towards a tall distinctive rock. Within 20m pick up a clear wide rocky path which passes a few metres to the right of the ROCK and heads down into the valley. From here on your route is clear.

After a fairly rough descent (take care, it's ankle twisting terrain), the valley narrows and you find yourself on its left-hand side. A flimsy GATE (**1h41min**) marks the start of a pleasant level path lined with colourful gorse. Keep your eyes open for ibex and deer on the slopes, but don't forget to duck to avoid pine branches that overhang the path. The **Llano del Endrinal**, a pine-covered meadow where they used to grow cereal crops, soon comes into view below, situated at the foot of the sheer cliffs of Peñón Grande (**1h52min**). Reach it after a short descent through rocks to a TROUGH and a deep WELL nearby (**1h56min**). Take the narrow path which rounds the meadow and head up to a little JUNCTION (**2h01min**). Fork left and left again, directly towards **Peñón Grande**, home to booted eagles, which you'll see soaring around here from March to September.

At the top of the rise, the flat-topped mountain in the distance is the appropriately-named Las Mesas (the Tables), and Ronda the town on its near side. As the path bears right and descends steeply again, Grazalema and its separate Villa Turistica appear below (**2h09min**). Cross a gentler area of rocks and pines and then a long-disused *era* (**2h25min**), before going through another rickety GATE (**2h31min**). Walk between fences and pass a very rustic old *cortijo* to the left, then reach the boundary fence of **Camping Tajo Rodillo**. Go round it to the left and descend to your starting point on the road, just above **Grazalema** (**2h36min**).

22 BENAOCAZ • CASA DEL DORNAJO • PUERTO BOYAR • SALTO DEL CABRERO • BENAOCAZ

Map pages 130-131   **Distance:** 18km/11.2mi; 6h20min

Grade: strenuous, but not difficult, with ascents and corresponding descents of 500m/1640ft overall.

Equipment : See page 51; *walking boots and compass essential.*

How to get there and return: 🚌 to/from Benaocaz (the 52km-point on Car tour 7); park in the village and make your way to the church.

Short walks: Equipment as page 51; access as main walk.

1 **Arroyo del Pajarito** (4km/2.5mi; 1h18min). Easy, despite the ascent and corresponding descent of 210m/690ft. Follow the main walk to the DYKE (28min). Do not go through the gate, but walk along the dyke to the left and scramble through a GAP IN THE STONE WALL ahead. Turn right up a narrow earthen path, following a FENCE up to a GAP IN ANOTHER STONE WALL. Several narrow paths, really just animal tracks, fan out from here across a rocky meadow. Take a central one and bear left across the middle of the meadow towards trees and a line of rocks at the other side (about 200m away). The tall rock at the end of the line leans to the left, and this is the way you must go, just before reaching it. Walk down the GRASSY SLOPE (35min) and as it ends, step down right, on to the start of a rocky PATH (39min). As it passes through an overgrown section, you'll cross a little STREAM BED and both see and hear the Arroyo del Pajarito far below on the right. Follow one of several paths, again mostly animal trails, which follow its direction downstream. Pass an animal TROUGH (46min) and come to the start of a long wall of rock. Follow the path, now clear, through an area of gorse, brilliantly coloured for many months of the year, and enjoy spectacular views across to the sierras in the far distance. The little conical huts of Los Chozos (hotel/apartments) appear down to the right, and then the rural plain below Benaocaz opens up. Reach the outskirts of the village at the **Refugio de Montaña El Parral** (1h09min) and carry straight on to the CHURCH (1h18min).

2 **Salto del Cabrero** (7.5km/4.7mi; 2h38min). Easy, with ascents and corresponding descents of 180m/590ft. This is the end of the main walk, in reverse. From the CHURCH make your way along the main street to the north end of the village, where you'll find the **Apartamentos San Anton** in a little square. Pass to the left of this building and, after going through a GATE, descend the cobbled trail, to cross the little stone bridge across the **Arroyo del Pajarito** (24min, *P*22). Follow the path as it continues through another GATE and passes alongside a DYKE in a grassy field (34min). Cross the field and start climbing on a winding, rocky trail, steep and sometimes cobbled. Go through a GATE (44min) and, at the top of the trail (56min), you'll see Cortijo del Puerto about 300m over to your right. The path continues through an area of gorse and rocks, goes through a GAP IN A DYKE and carries on across a grassy meadow (1h10min). Looking to your left, you will see the *salto*, your goal, through a gap in the sierra. Access is through a gap in the dyke, where a rocky path takes you down to the **Salto del Cabrero** (1h19min). Now pick up the main walk at the 4h-point to return to Benaocaz by the same route.

Alternative walk: From Benaocaz to Grazalema (11.5km/7.1mi; 3h48min). Strenuous, with an ascent of 500m/1640ft and descent of 470m/1540ft. Equipment as for main walk. Access: Plan this as either a morning or afternoon walk. If you walk in the morning, park in Benaocaz and return from Grazalema on the lunchtime 🚐 (Timetable 11). If you walk in the afternoon, park in Grazalema and take the lunchtime 🚐 from there to Benaocaz (Timetable 11) to start the walk. Follow the main walk to the 2h30min-point and locate the cairn on top of a tall rock. Then pick up *Walk 21* at the 1h18min-point and follow it to Grazalema.

Ruins of an old farm, a mountain pass and a geological rarity are just a few of the features of interest on this long and varied walk. Cattle roam across much of the terrain, so you'll encounter an unusual number of gates, some makeshift, some substantial, and walls. These latter, in various stages of repair, are drystone dykes, constructed from the rocks which are strewn in abundance over the grassy surface of the whole region. In some places, like the Llano de las Presillas, the rocks and boulders have been strangely moulded by the elements.

Start out from the CHURCH: walk along the street past the 'Tabacos'. Turn left and, passing the CROSS, cut diagonally right into Puente Alcolea. Take the cobbled trail which goes up to the left just before a RUINED HOUSE (**3min**). It climbs gradually between smallholdings, running parallel to the Sierra del Caillo ridge which stretches into the distance on the right. Fork left before a TROUGH and *fuente,* and go through the first GATE (**10min**) onto open slopes. The trail bends right and upwards, soon passing through a creaky METAL GATE. As it narrows and becomes a clear path, follow it up the valley between gorse and olive trees.

Pass between large rocks to an open area with a gate in the dyke diagonally to the right (**28min**). Walk through the GATE, now on a wider path. *(But for Short walk 1, go left without passing through the gate.)* Pitted from the constant pounding of cattle hooves, the ground is considerably eroded, but delicate little wildflowers still manage to survive in profusion.

Some stone ANIMAL PENS are tucked in at the foot of the rocky slope on the left (**41min**), before the path bears right into a dip. Pass through TWO GATES, the first a Heath Robinson affair, the second a rather more substantial one which opens into a stream. Head slightly left and upwards through more olive trees and gorse, the path becoming rocky and clearer as you proceed.

Pass through a GAP IN A DYKE (**54min**) and follow the path to the left. The Sierra del Caillo ridge, rugged and barren, is in stark contrast to the delightful valley it protects. Soon coming into view ahead is a man-made structure, the *fuente* which serves Casa Fardela, a little way beyond it. The land round the house is fenced off so, about 20 metres before the *fuente,* go through the GATE in the fence on the left (**1h04min**). You can just see **Casa Fardela** from here.

Go up the grassy slope and veer right, to pick up a fairly clear path which takes you round the boundary and heads back towards the ridge (look out here for vultures soaring above you). From a little GULLY (**1h15min**) an animal trough can be seen about 50 metres ahead, and Casa Fardela is down to the right, now just out of sight beyond the wall. From the gully turn sharp left noticing, about 200 metres ahead, a conical mass of limestone with a sheer and jagged rock 'wall' stretching to its left and just visible above the trees.

Casa Fardela

Strike out through rocks and trees — there's no real path, just animal trails — making for the left-hand end of the 'wall' of rock. As you get closer, you'll pick up a clear path which takes you through a GATE (**1h24min**) to the other side of the 'wall'.

From here your clear path bears right, circling round the slopes and gradually descending. When it appears to end, just carry on across rocks, to pick it up again as it continues round and descends past a *fuente* and some stone-walled *corales*, animal enclosures (**1h30min**). Beyond these lie the substantial ruins of an old farm, **Casa del Dornajo**, magnificently situated before a backdrop of the twin peaks of Simancón and Reloj. Just before reaching the house (**1h35min**), look across to the left and locate the grassy tree-covered *collado* you'll be walking alongside later. Have a break and take some time to explore here.

Your onward route passes between the HOUSE and a HUGE DEAD TREE, heading northeast towards a stand of tall poplars. About 20 metres to the left of the poplars, look for a CAIRN (**1h39min**) which signals your continuing path. It is rocky and initially follows the same direction, but it soon veers left and circles round the rocky slopes, with welcome shade provided by occasional evergreeen oaks. There are some BLUE PAINT WAYMARKINGS along the route, usually faded, and directed back the way you have just come. Steadily gaining altitude, you pass through a GAP IN A DYKE (**2h06min**). The path goes straight ahead, then bears right to descend, steeply in places, along the side of the *collado* previously located. Go up through the GATE IN THE DYKE at the head of the *collado* (**2h25min**) and carry straight on, heading north, on an indistinct path across **Llano de las Presillas**. Isolated and remote though it feels, one Sunday we encountered three other groups of walkers up here.

As the path approaches what appears to be a barrier of rocks ahead, notice a CAIRN on top of a tall rock to the right (**2h30min**). (*This marks the start of a path which takes the Alternative walk and Walk 21 down to Grazalema.*) The main walk continues straight ahead, with a CAIRN OR TWO to mark the way. As the vegetation increases, the path becomes clearer and pebbly, and you start descending (**2h40min**). Down below, a valley opens out, and you'll see the road running through the Puerto del Boyar, a pass at 1103m. Wind steeply down to the valley floor and follow the path as it bears right, through a level stretch of pines and rocks (**2h51min**; *P*21).

At the far end, where the earth is churned up with

animal tracks, the path turns left and becomes rocky as it descends, steeply at first, to reach a gully. You'll see the beginnings of the Río Guadalete here and the gate ahead takes you out to the road at the *merendero*, stone picnic shelter, a little below the layby at the **Puerto del Boyar (3h)**.

Walk a few metres up the wide path past the *merendero*, then go through a GATE signposted for the Salto del Cabrero. From here, a track takes you through pines, with views into the Llano del Boyar, a deep valley to the right. After you go through another GATE (**3h08min**), the Salto del Cabrero (Goatherd's Leap) is clearly visible ahead, but still a long way off. In the immediate distance lies a working *cortijo*, the **Cortijo de las Albarradas**. Just before you reach it, GREEN ARROWS (**3h26min**) direct you left off the track and lead you through a GATE alongside animal pens. The path, with a few markings at first, takes you through the middle of a narrow green valley. The trees attract many birds, and you'll hardly fail to catch a flash of colour as a redstart flies across your path.

The slope begins to drop away on the right, and the path runs along the foot of the steep rocky slopes on the left, descending a little (**3h46min**) to meet a FENCE. There's no way through the fence at this point, so the path veers right and through a GATE a little further downhill, before returning to run close to the cliffs again. Descend gradually through glorious woodland and cross a WATERCOURSE (**4h01min**), which could be torrential or dry depending on the season. Head uphill, to pass through another GATE (**4h09min**). Then take the right-hand fork and cross a little grassy clearing. Poking out from amongst the rocks ahead is the chimney of the **Cortijo de la Fuentezuela** and just beyond the little house is its *fuente* (**4h13min**).

Turn up left here on a steep clear narrow path which takes you on to a plateau where goats and cattle roam and rocks have been gathered into heaps to ensure sufficient grazing (**4h26min**). Vultures patrol the ridge to the left, so keep your eyes open as you follow the path past the **Cortijo del Santo** and to a DYKE (**4h35min**). Climb over the dyke and follow it downhill to the right. At the end, pick up a path going left, which leads to a GATE (**4h39min**).

Pass through yet another area of rocks and gorse, noticing a meadow down to the right. Beyond it, through a gap in the sierra, you'll see the valley below. Soon (**4h 41min**) head off right through rocks and gorse down to the meadow — there isn't a clear path, but it doesn't matter. Cross the meadow and go through a GAP IN A DYKE, where a rocky path descends straight ahead. The path takes you just alongside the **Salto del Cabrero** (**5h**), which opens up on the right — almost too close for comfort. Take in this amazing natural phenomenon, picking your vantage point and being careful of the sheer drops.

Retrace your steps to the meadow (**5h09min**) and head right, picking up a path at the end of the meadow. It rises through rocks and a DYKE and continues across a rocky plateau, picking its way between gorse bushes. The Sierra del Caillo is clear ahead, and Benaocaz comes into view (**5h18min**). Soon you'll notice the **Cortijo del Puerto** at the **Puerto Don Fernando** (**5h23min**), set off the path about 300m to the left. Twice a day the goats are milked up here, and the churns filled and carried back by convoys of donkeys and mules to the villages.

The path becomes a rocky trail, steep and sometimes cobbled, which zigzags down to a GATE (**5h35min**). Pass through and, on reaching a narrow grassy field (**5h45min**), turn right along a DYKE at the far side. Go through another GATE (**5h49min**) and continue down to a tiny stone bridge across the bubbling **Arroyo del Pajarito** (**5h55min**; *P*22).

A cobbled trail takes you through a GATE and past the first of the worksheds and houses on the outskirts of **Benaocaz** (**5h56min**). Pass (and ignore) a confusing information panel and walk along the main street of the village to the CHURCH (**6h20min**).

23 RIO EL BOSQUE

See photograph page 46 and map pages 130-131

Distance: 10km/6.2mi; 2h55min

Grade: Easy, but on a short stretch where steep rocks reach right down to the waterside, you must negotiate a narrow stepped path that has been hewn out about a metre above the water. Descent and corresponding ascent of 140m/460ft.

Equipment: see page 51.

How to get there and return: 🚌 to/from the 75km-point on Car tour 7. Turn left and drive about half a kilometre down the tree-lined road towards Benamahoma. Park beside the bus stop, just before a bar at the entrance to the village. Except on Sundays, it is possible to catch the afternoon bus from El Bosque back to Benamahoma if you do not wish to walk both ways (Timetable 12).

Lose yourself in the beauty and freshness of the shady woodland canopy as you follow this typical riverside path downstream, then back again. It is often ablaze with wildflowers and, in the trees, you will hear nightingales, tits, warblers and woodpeckers. Dippers prefer to perch on rocks in the fast-flowing water, home to trout, otters and other aquatic creatures. In former times the power of the water was harnessed by several woollen mills, now in ruins. This walk can be enjoyed at any time of the year and, combined with a leisurely lunch in El Bosque, makes a perfect day out.

The walk starts by the BRIDGE, just a few metres from the bus stop. An INFORMATION PANEL provides historical detail and a 'Camino El Bosque' sign directs you left. Cross a stream on STEPPING-STONES and reach the riverside path, immediately relinquishing the sounds of habitation for the song of birds. Cross two little bridges over streams but ignore one which crosses the river, keeping it on your right. Where the path splits, you have the choice of passing above or below the FIRST OF THE RUINED MILLS (**10min**) and, shortly afterwards, a long flat grassy area with another MILL up on the bank provides a good spot for a pause (**14min**; *P*23). Beyond more ruins (**21min**), pass a bridge where an amusing notice encourages you to take your litter home (**24min**).

When several narrow paths fan out, keep to the highest and, as the banks close in, the main path becomes quite rocky and undulating for a while. Reach the FIRST BRIDGE (**33min**) of several which takes the path back and forth across the river. An *acequia* is just visible above a rock fall, shortly before a three-section bridge across an attractive open area of shallow WATERFALLS AND POOLS (**41min**). The next stretch is the tricky bit. Just take care as you make your way round the rocks.

139

Pass another rubbish notice board shortly before the white building of the *fábrica de la luz* (hydroelectric plant) comes into sight on the opposite bank (**51min**). It used to be served by the *acequia,* but ceased operating in 1963. A track leads away from here and goes to the road, but you fork down right after just a few metres, to a path by the waterside. There's an interesting FAUNA INFORMATION PANEL (**56min**) just before you cross the river again, this time to a cultivated meadow with eucalyptus trees beyond it. After a pleasant level stroll along its edge you'll see across the river the partially-renovated **Molino de Arriba** (Upper Mill; **1h08min**). Its St Bernard dogs love to bark at passers-by from the opposite bank.

After the path crosses a wide TRACK (**1h11min**) and then a little BRIDGE over a stream, a 'Peligro Ganado Bravo' (Danger Fierce Cattle) notice on a gate on the right is one of several in the area, erected by locals to keep casual walkers off their property. But it does not affect you, as the path continues past it, with El Bosque soon coming into view (**1h18min**). Pass some market gardens just before the large trout hatchery which sits below the village. A small BRIDGE (**1h25min**) takes you to its boundary fence to allow a closer look. Continue to the ROAD (**1h28min**) and cross a bridge to the **Molino de Enmedio** (Middle Mill); this has been converted into a youth hostel. A convenient restaurant, not surprisingly, offers trout as its speciality.

The walk turns back here, but it's worth tackling the very steep slope up into the village of **El Bosque**, where there is a BOTANICAL GARDEN and a VISITOR CENTRE. The bus back to Benamahoma leaves from the main square, but you'll find that returning along the riverside to your car at **Benama-homa** (**2h55min**) is just as pleasant as the outward walk.

BUS AND TRAIN TIMETABLES

TRAINS
1 Málaga—Torremolinos—Benalmádena—Fuengirola
A fast, efficient train service leaves central Málaga (near the big department store El Corte Inglés) every half-hour.
Journey time Marbella—Fuengirola: 42 minutes

BUSES
2 Marbella—Fuengirola—Torremolinos—Málaga (along the coast)
Regular bus service, approximately half-hourly to hourly (depending on time of day), including Sundays (07.00-22.30).
Journey time Marbella—Málaga about 1h15min

3 Málaga—Torre del Mar—Nerja—Cueva de Nerja (along the coast)
Regular bus service, approximately hourly (depending on time of day), including Sundays (07.00-21.30).
Journey time Málaga—Nerja about 1h30min

4 Capileira—Pampaneira *(for Walk 4)*
Departs Capileira 15.50, 18.20. *Journey time 10 minutes*

5 Frigiliana—Nerja *(for Walk 11); no service Sundays or holidays*
Departs Frigiliana 07.00 08.00 10.30 12.45 14.00 16.30 19.30
Departs Nerja   07.15 09.30 12.00 13.30 14.45 19.00 20.30

6 Torre del Mar—Puente Don Manuel—Ventas de Zafarraya *(for Walk 13)*
Departs Torre del Mar 08.00, 11.00 (Alsina Graells red bus or Jimenez white minibus to Granada); passes Puente Don Manuel 08.30, 11.30. Departs Puente Don Manuel 13.00 and 16.30 (Jimenez); 17.30 (Alsina Graells). *Times are approximate — be early!*

7 Fuengirola—Mijas *(for Walk 15)*
Buses each day (08.00 to 22.00) in either direction, approximately every half hour.
Journey time 20 minutes

8 Fuengirola—Entrerrios *(for Walk 16)*
Autobuses Urbanos Linea 3, departs from outside the Mercacentro in Fuengirola.
Departs Fuengirola 07.35, 13.20.
Departs the Albergue Municipal at Entrerrios 1350, 1905.
Journey time 20 minutes

9 Ojén—Marbella *(for Walk 17)* — *no service Sundays or holidays*
Departs Ojén 06.30 07.30 08.30 10.15 14.00 (not Sat), 15.15 (not Sat), 16.15 17.15 18.45 19.45 20.45.

10 Marbella—Istán *(for Walk 18)*
Autocares Perez, departs the Edificio Pentágono, outside the bus station in Marbella.
Departs Marbella   08.00 14.30 19.00. Sundays and holidays 14.00 19.00
Departs Istán   07.15 09.00 17.00. Sundays and holidays 09.00 16.00

Continues overleaf

11 Ronda—Grazalema—Benaocaz—Ubrique: Los Amarillos buses
(for Walks 21 and 22)

	Mon to Fri		Sat		Sun, fiestas	
Ronda	12.00	17.45	12.30	17.15	12.30	17.15
Grazalema	13.00	18.45	13.30	18.15	13.30	18.15
Benaocaz	13.20	19.05	13.50	18.35	13.50	18.35
Ubrique	13.30	19.15	14.00	18.45	14.00	18.45
Ubrique	07.30	15.30	06.30	15.30	08.30	15.30
Benaocaz	07.40*	15.40*	06.40*	15.40*	08.40*	15.40*
Grazalema	08.00	16.00	07.00	16.00	09.00	16.00
Ronda	09.00	17.00	08.00	17.00	10.00	17.00

*Benaocaz times are approximate — arrive early!

12 El Bosque—Benamahoma—Puerto del Boyar—Grazalema
(for Walk 23); no service on Sundays or holidays

	Mon-Fri		Fridays only	Saturdays
El Bosque	06.45	15.15	19.30	16.00
Benamahoma	06.55	15.25	19.40	16.10
Puerto del Boyar	07.10	15.40	19.55	16.25
Grazalema	07.15	15.45	20.00	16.30

Intermediate times are all approximate — be early!